Quiz: 87548

ARv
8.2
pts.
1.0

DATE DUE

Eyewitness
WORLD WAR I

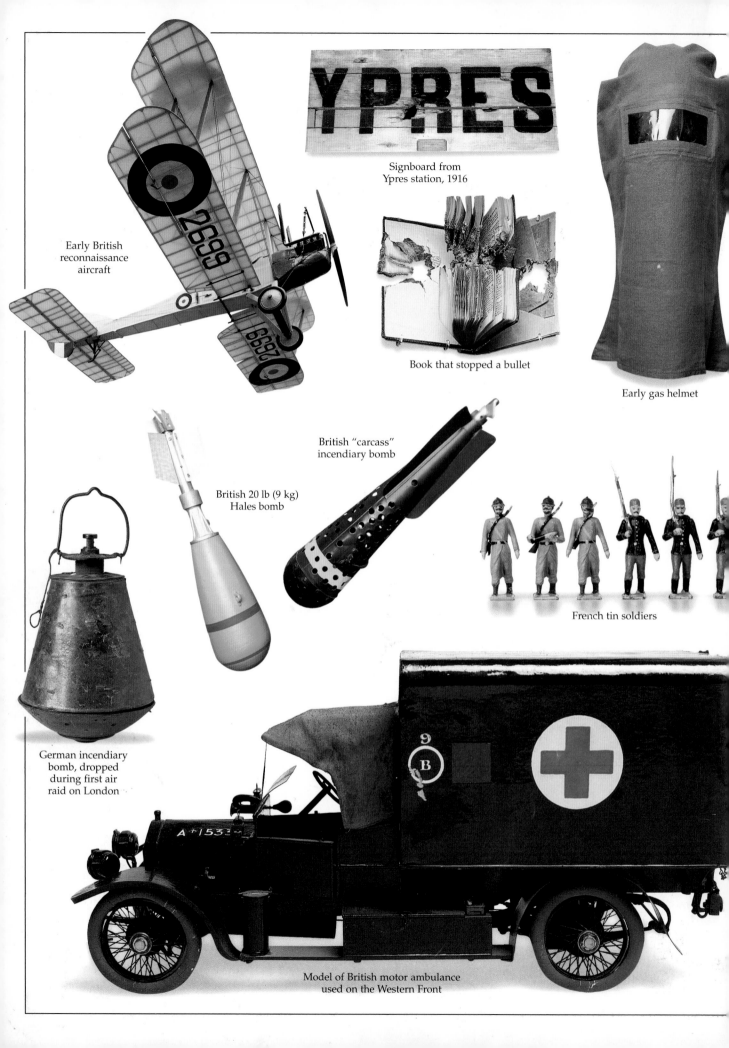

Early British
reconnaissance
aircraft

Signboard from
Ypres station, 1916

Book that stopped a bullet

Early gas helmet

British "carcass"
incendiary bomb

British 20 lb (9 kg)
Hales bomb

French tin soldiers

German incendiary
bomb, dropped
during first air
raid on London

Model of British motor ambulance
used on the Western Front

Prussian Iron
Cross

Eyewitness

WORLD
WAR I

American
Distinguished
Service Cross

Written by
SIMON ADAMS

Photographed by
ANDY CRAWFORD

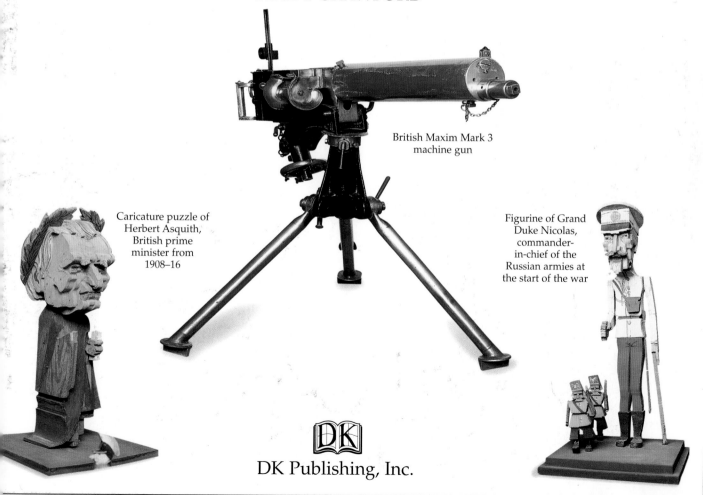

British Maxim Mark 3
machine gun

Caricature puzzle of
Herbert Asquith,
British prime
minister from
1908–16

Figurine of Grand
Duke Nicolas,
commander-
in-chief of the
Russian armies at
the start of the war

[DK]
DK Publishing, Inc.

British officer's compass

French *Croix de Guerre* medal awarded for valor

DK

LONDON, NEW YORK,
MELBOURNE, MUNICH, and DELHI

Project editor Patricia Moss
Art editors Julia Harris, Rebecca Painter
Senior editor Monica Byles
Senior art editors Jane Tetzlaff, Clare Shedden
Category publisher Jayne Parsons
Managing art editor Jacquie Gulliver
Senior production controller Kate Oliver
Picture research Sean Hunter
DTP designers Justine Eaton, Matthew Ibbotson

REVISED EDITION
Managing editors Linda Esposito, Camilla Hallinan
Managing art editors Jane Thomas, Martin Wilson
Publishing manager Sunita Gahir
Category publisher Andrea Pinnington
Senior editor Shaila Awan
Editors Clare Hibbert, Sue Nicholson
Art director Simon Webb
Art editor Rebecca Johns
Production Jenny Jacoby, Georgina Hayworth
Picture research Sean Hunter
DTP designers Siu Chan, Andy Hilliard, Ronaldo Julien

U.S. editor Elizabeth Hester
Senior editor Beth Sutinis
Art editor Dirk Kaufman
U.S. production Chris Avgherinos
U.S. DTP designer Milos Orlovic

This Eyewitness ® Guide has been conceived by
Dorling Kindersley Limited and Editions Gallimard

This edition first published in the United States in 2007
by DK Publishing, Inc.,
375 Hudson Street,
New York, New York 10014

Copyright © 2001, © 2004, © 2007 Dorling Kindersley Limited

07 08 10 9 8 7 6 5 4 3 2 1
HD118 - 04/07

A catalog record for this book is available from
the Library of Congress.

ISBN 978-0-7566-3007-2 (HC) 978-0-7566-0741-8 (Library Binding)

Color reproduction by Colourscan, Singapore
Printed in China by Toppan Printing Co., (Shenzhen) Ltd.

Discover more at

www.dk.com

German steel helmet adapted for use with a telephone

Dummy rifles used by British army recruits, 1914–15

British and German barbed wire

British steel helmet with viso

Grenade

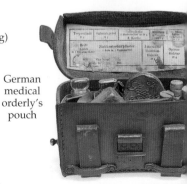

German medical orderly's pouch

Contents

High-explosive shells

Divided Europe

AT THE START of the 20th century, the countries of Europe were increasingly hostile to each other. Britain, France, and Germany competed for trade and influence overseas, while Austria-Hungary and Russia both tried to dominate the Balkan states of southeast Europe. Military tension between Germany and Austria-Hungary on the one hand and Russia and France on the other led to the formation of powerful military alliances. A naval arms race added to the tension. In 1912-13, two major wars broke out in the Balkans as rival states battled to divide Turkish-controlled lands between them. By 1914, the political situation in Europe was tense, but few believed that a continental war was inevitable.

HMS *DREADNOUGHT*
The launch of HMS *Dreadnought* in February 1906 marked a revolution in battleship design. With its 10 12-inch (30-cm) guns and a top speed of 21 knots, the British ship outperformed and outpaced every other battleship of the day. As a result, Germany, France, and other maritime nations began to design and build their own "Dreadnoughts," starting a worldwide naval armaments race.

KAISER WILHELM II
Wilhelm II became emperor of Germany in 1888, when he was just 29. He had a withered arm and other disabilities, but overcame them through his strong personality. As emperor, he tried to turn Germany from a European power into a world power, but his aggressive policies and arrogant behavior upset other European nations, particularly Britain and France.

Some children had models of HMS Dreadnought and could recite every detail of her statistics

Hand-painted, tinplate toy battleship

EUROPEAN RIVALRIES

In 1882, Germany, Austria-Hungary, and Italy formed the Triple Alliance to protect themselves against invasion. Alarmed by this, France and Russia formed an alliance in 1894. Britain signed ententes (understandings) with France in 1904 and Russia in 1907. During the war, Serbia, Montenegro, Belgium, Romania, Portugal, and Greece fought with the Allies. Bulgaria and Turkey fought alongside Germany and Austria-Hungary – the Central Powers. Italy joined the Allies in 1915.

Central Powers

Allied Nations

Neutral

A FAMILY AFFAIR?
Although George V and Czar Nicholas II look very similar, they were not directly related. Nicholas's wife, Alexandra, however, was a cousin of George V, as was Emperor Wilhelm of Germany.

Czar Nicholas II of Russia   George V of Britain

THE GERMAN FLEET
In 1898, Germany began an ambitious naval building program designed to challenge the supremacy of the British Royal Navy. While German admirals commanded these new ships in the Baltic and North seas, German children played with tin battleships in their bathtubs.

Key to wind-up motor

THE POWER HOUSE
The factory, shown above, in the Ruhr valley of western Germany belonged to the Alfred Krupp Arms Company. The Krupp family was the largest arms supplier in the world. Germany was a largely agricultural nation when it became a united country in 1871. Over the next 30 years, new iron, coal, steel, engineering, and shipbuilding industries turned Germany into the third biggest industrial country in the world, after the US and Britain, which were the largest.

The fatal shot

ON JUNE 28, 1914, the heir to the Austro-Hungarian throne, Archduke Franz Ferdinand, was assassinated in Sarajevo, Bosnia. Bosnia had been part of Austria-Hungary since 1908, but it was claimed by neighboring Serbia. Austria-Hungary blamed Serbia for the assassination, and on July 28 declared war. What began as the third Balkan war within two years turned into a European war. Russia supported Serbia, Germany supported Austria-Hungary, and France supported Russia. On August 4, Germany invaded neutral Belgium on its way to France. It intended to knock France out of the war before turning its attention to Russia, thus avoiding war on two fronts. But Britain had guaranteed to defend Belgium's neutrality, and it too declared war on Germany. The Great War had begun.

MOBILIZE!
During July 1914, military notices were posted up across Europe informing citizens that their country's army was being mobilized (prepared) for war and that all those belonging to regular and reserve forces should report for duty.

THE AUSTRO-HUNGARIAN ARMY
The Austro-Hungarian empire had three armies – Austrian, Hungarian, and the "Common Army." Ten main languages were spoken! The official one was German, but officers had to learn their men's language, leading to frequent communication difficulties. The complex structure of the army reflected Austria-Hungary itself, which in reality was two separate monarchies ruled by one monarch.

GERMANY REJOICES
Germany prepared its army on August 1, declaring war against Russia later the same day and against France on August 3. Most Germans in the cities were enthusiastic for the war, and many civilians rushed to join the army in support of Kaiser and country. Germans in the countryside were less enthusiastic.

Austro-Hungarian *Reiter* (Trooper) of the 8th Uhlan (Lancer) Regiment

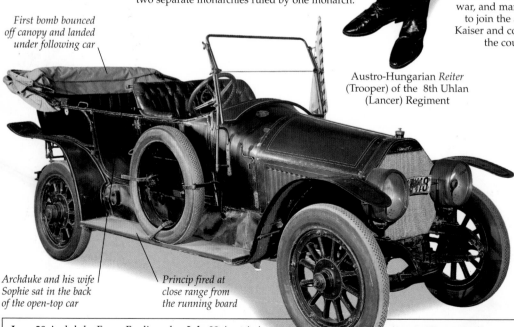

First bomb bounced off canopy and landed under following car

Archduke and his wife Sophie sat in the back of the open-top car

Princip fired at close range from the running board

ONE DAY IN SARAJE[VO]
The six assassins – five Serbs and [a] Bosnian Muslim – lay in wait al[ong] Archduke Ferdinand's route to [the] Austrian governor's residence [in] Sarajevo. One of them threw a bo[mb] at Ferdinand's car, but it bounced [off] and exploded under the following [car,] injuring two army officers. [The] Archduke and his wife went to v[isit] the injured officers in the hospita[l 30] minutes later. When their car too[k a] wrong turn, Gavrilo Princip stepp[ed] out of the crowd and shot the cou[ple.] Ferdinand's wife died instantly, [and] he died 10 minutes la[ter.]

June 28 Archduke Franz Ferdinand is assassinated in Sarajevo.
July 5 Germany gives its ally, Austria-Hungary, total support for any action it takes against Serbia.

July 23 Austria issues a drastic ultimatum to Serbia, which would undermine Serbian independence.
July 25 Serbia agrees to most of

Austria-Hungary's demands, but still mobilizes as a safety precaution.
July 28 Austria-Hungary ignores Serbia's readiness to seek a peaceful

end to the crisis and declares w[ar]
July 30 Russia mobilizes in sup[port] of its ally, Serbia.
July 31 Germany demands Rus[sia] stops its mobilization

Bekanntmachung.

Mobilmachung befohlen.

Erster Mobilmachungstag, der 2. August

Vorstehender Allerhöchster Befehl wird hierdurch öffentlich bekannt gemacht.

Berlin, den 1. August 1914.

Der Oberbürgermeister
Wermuth.

German (above) and French (right) mobilization posters

ARMÉE DE TERRE ET ARMÉE DE MER

ORDRE
DE MOBILISATION GÉNÉRALE

Par décret du Président de la République, la mobilisation des armées de terre et de mer est ordonnée, ainsi que la réquisition des animaux, voitures et harnais nécessaires au complément de ces armées.

Le premier jour de la mobilisation est le *Dimanche deux Août 1914*

Tout Français soumis aux obligations militaires doit, sous peine d'être puni avec toute rigueur des lois, obéir aux prescriptions du **FASCICULE DE MOBILISATION** (pages colorées placées dans son livret).

Sont visés par le présent ordre **TOUS LES HOMMES** non présents sous les Drapeaux et appartenant :

1° à l'ARMÉE DE TERRE y compris les **TROUPES COLONIALES** et les hommes des **SERVICES AUXILIAIRES** ;

2° à l'ARMÉE DE MER y compris les **INSCRITS MARITIMES** et les **ARMURIERS DE LA MARINE**.

VIVE LA FRANCE
The French army mobilized on August 1. For many Frenchmen, the war was an opportunity to seek revenge for the German defeat of France in 1870–71 and the loss of Alsace-Lorraine to German control.

ALL ABOARD!
The German slogans on this westbound train read "Daytrip to Paris" and "See you again on the Boulevard," as all Germans believed that their offensive against France would soon take them to Paris. French trains heading east toward Germany carried similar messages about Berlin.

> *"The lamps are going out all over Europe"*
>
> SIR EDWARD GREY
> BRITISH FOREIGN SECRETARY, 1914

ust 1 Germany mobilizes
[against] Russia and declares war;
[Fran]ce mobilizes in support of its
[ally] Russia; Germany signs a
[treat]y with Ottoman Turkey; Italy
declares its neutrality.
August 2 Germany invades Luxembourg and demands the right to enter neutral Belgium, which is refused.

August 3 Germany declares war on France.
August 4 Germany invades Belgium on route to France; Britain enters the war to safeguard
Belgian neutrality.
August 6 Austria-Hungary declares war on Russia.
August 12 France and Britain declare war on Austria-Hungary.

War in the west

CHRISTMAS TREAT
The London Territorial Association sent each of their soldiers a "Christmas pudding" in 1914. Other soldiers received gifts in the name of Princess Mary, daughter of King George V.

Ever since the 1890s, Germany had feared that it would face a war on two fronts – against Russia in the east and against France, Russia's ally since 1894, in the west. Germany knew the chances of winning such a war were slim. By 1905, the chief of the German staff, Field Marshal Count Alfred von Schlieffen, had developed a bold plan to knock France swiftly out of any war before turning the full might of the German army against Russia. For this plan to work, the German army had to pass through Belgium, a neutral country. In August 1914, the plan went into operation. German troops crossed the Belgian border on August 4, and by the end of the month, invaded northern France. The Schlieffen Plan then required the army to sweep around the north and west of Paris, but the German commander, General Moltke, modified the plan and instead headed east of Paris. This meant his right flank (side) was exposed to the French and British armies. At the Battle of the Marne on September 5, the German advance was held and pushed back. By Christmas 1914, the two sides faced a stalemate along a line from the Belgian coast in the north to the Swiss border in the south.

IN RETREAT
The Belgian army was too s[...] and inexperienced to resist [...] invading German army. He[...] soldiers with dog-drawn machine guns are withdraw[n] to Antwerp.

Third gunner fires the gun on command

Second gunner loads the shell

First gunner hands shell to second gunner on command

IN THE FIELD
The British Expeditionary Force (BEF) had arrived in France by August 22, 1914. Its single cavalry division included members of the Royal Horse Artillery, whose L Battery fired this 13-pounder quick-firing Mark I gun against the German 4th Cavalry Division at the Battle of Néry on September 1. This held up the German advance into France for one morning. Three gunners in the battery received Victoria Crosses for their valor.

Steel helmet

Shaft to attach gun to horses that pull the gun

Soldiers wore puttees, long strips of cloth wrapped around their legs

THE CHRISTMAS TRUCE

On Christmas Eve 1914, soldiers on both sides of the Western Front sung carols to each other in comradely greeting. The following day, troops along two-thirds of the front observed a truce. All firing stopped, and church services were held. A few soldiers crossed into no-man's-land to talk to their enemy and exchange simple gifts of cigarettes and other items. Near Ploegsteert Wood, south of Ypres, Belgium, a game of soccer took place between members of the German Royal Saxon Regiment and the Scottish Seaforth Highlanders. The Germans won 3–2. In some places, the truce lasted for almost a week. A year later, however, sentries on both sides were ordered to shoot anyone attempting a repeat performance.

Soldier shooting at enemy with a note saying "Christmas Eve – Get em!"

British and German soldiers greeting each other on Christmas Day

EYEWITNESS

Captain E.R.P. Berryman, of the 2nd Battalion 39th Garwhal Rifles, wrote a letter home describing the truce. He told his family that the Germans had put up Christmas trees in their trenches. This cartoon illustrates the absurdity of his situation – shooting the enemy one day and greeting them as friends the next.

German trench

Rope wrapped around recoil mechanism

Fires 12.5-lb (5.6-kg) shells a distance of 5,900 yd (5,395 m)

HEADING FOR THE FRONT

The German advance into northern France was so rapid that by early September, its troops were along the Marne River, only 25 miles (40 km) east of Paris. General Gallieni, military governor of Paris, took 600 taxis and used them to convey 6,000 men to the front line to reinforce the French 6th Army.

Fighting men

THE OUTBREAK OF WAR in Europe in August 1914 changed the lives of millions of men. Regular soldiers, older reservists, eager recruits, and unwilling conscripts all found themselves caught up in the war. Some of them were experienced soldiers, but many had barely held a rifle before. In addition to the European forces, both Britain and France drew heavily on armies recruited from their overseas colonies and from the British dominions. The design and detail of their uniforms differed considerably, although brighter colors soon gave way to khaki, dull blue, and gray.

France

Hat flaps could be pulled down to keep out the cold

Jerkin cou[ld] made of go[at] or sheepsk[in]

Ammunition pouch

GRAND DUKE NICOLAS
At the outbreak of war, the Russian army was led by Grand Duke Nicolas, uncle of Czar Nicholas II. In August 1915, the czar dismissed his uncle and took command himself. As commander-in-chief, the czar dealt with the overall strategy of the war. The Russian armies were led by generals who directed the battles. The other warring countries employed similar chains of command.

THE BRITISH ARMY
At the start of war, the British army contained 247,432 regulars and 218,280 reservists. Soldiers wore a khaki uniform consisting of a single-breasted tunic with a folding collar, trousers, puttees or leggings worn to protect the shins, and ankle-boots. In the winter, soldiers were issued with additional items such as jerkins. Many wore knitted scarves and balaclavas sent from home.

Lee Enfield Rifle

Woole[n] puttee[s] wrapp[ed] aroun[d] shins

Britis[h] soldie[r]

Thick boo[ts] to protect

Russia

EMPIRE TROOPS
The British and French armies included large numbers of recruits from their colonial possessions in Africa, Asia, the Pacific, and the Caribbean. In addition, the British dominions of Australia, New Zealand, Canada, and South Africa sent their own armies to take part in the conflict. Many of these troops had never left their home countries before. These Annamites (Indo-Chinese), above from French Indo-China were stationed with the French army at Salonika, Greece, in 1916. They wore their own uniforms rather than those of the French army.

EASTERN ALLIES
In Eastern Europe, Germany faced the vast Russian army, as well as smaller armies from Serbia and Montenegro. In the Far East, German colonies in China and the Pacific Ocean were invaded by Japan. These illustrations come from a poster showing Germany's enemies.

France

Britain

Belgium

Steel helmets
were issued
in 1916

Field tunic
(Waffenrock)

Tent cloth

ridge
·h

Mauser
rifle

Stick grenade

as
sk

German
soldier

THE GERMAN ARMY
The German army
was the strongest in
Europe because it had
been preparing for
war. At the outbreak
of hostilities, it
consisted of 840,000
men. All men under
the age of 45 were
trained for military
service and belonged
to the reserve army.
On calling up the
reserves, the German
army could expand to
over four million
trained men.

French infantrymen photographed in 1918

WESTERN ALLIES
In Western Europe, Britain,
France, and Belgium were
allied against Germany.
The British and French
armies were large, but the
Belgian army was small
and inexperienced. These
illustrations come from a
German poster identifying
the enemy.

THE FRENCH ARMY
The French army was one
of the largest in Europe.
Including reservists
and colonial troops, the
French army totaled
3,680,000 trained men
at the outbreak of war.

Water bottle

Haversack with
personal items

Lebel rifle

French infantryman,
known as *le poilu*

ussia

Serbia

Montenegro

Japan

Enlisting

AT THE OUTBREAK OF WAR, every European country but one had a large standing army of conscripted troops ready to fight. The exception was Britain, which had a small army made up of volunteers. On August 6, 1914, the Secretary of War, Lord Kitchener, asked for 100,000 new recruits. Whole streets and villages of patriotic men lined up to enlist. Most thought they would be home by Christmas. By the end of 1915, 2,446,719 men had volunteered, but more were needed to fill the depleted ranks of soldiers. In January 1916 conscription was introduced for all single men aged 18–41.

WAR LEADER
British Prime Minister Herbert Asquith was caricatured as "the last of the Romans" and replaced by David Lloyd George in December 1916.

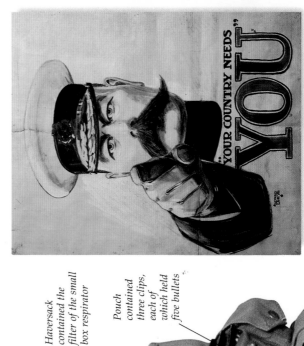

THE TEST
Every British recruit had to undergo a medical test to make sure he was fit to fight. Large numbers failed this test, because of poor eyesight, chest complaints, or general ill health. Others were refused because they were under 18, although many lied about their age. Once he passed the test, the recruit took the oath of loyalty to the king and was then accepted into the army.

"YOUR COUNTRY NEEDS YOU"
A portrait of British War Minister General Kitchener was used as a recruiting poster. By the [...]

Small box respirator gas mask

Haversack contained the filter of the small box respirator

Pouch contained three clips, each of which held five bullets

Two sets of five

LINE UP HERE FOR KING AND COUNTRY
At the outbreak of war, long lines formed at recruiting offices around the country. Men from the same area or industry grouped together to form the famous Pals battllions, so they could fight together. By mid-September, half a million men had volunteered to fight.

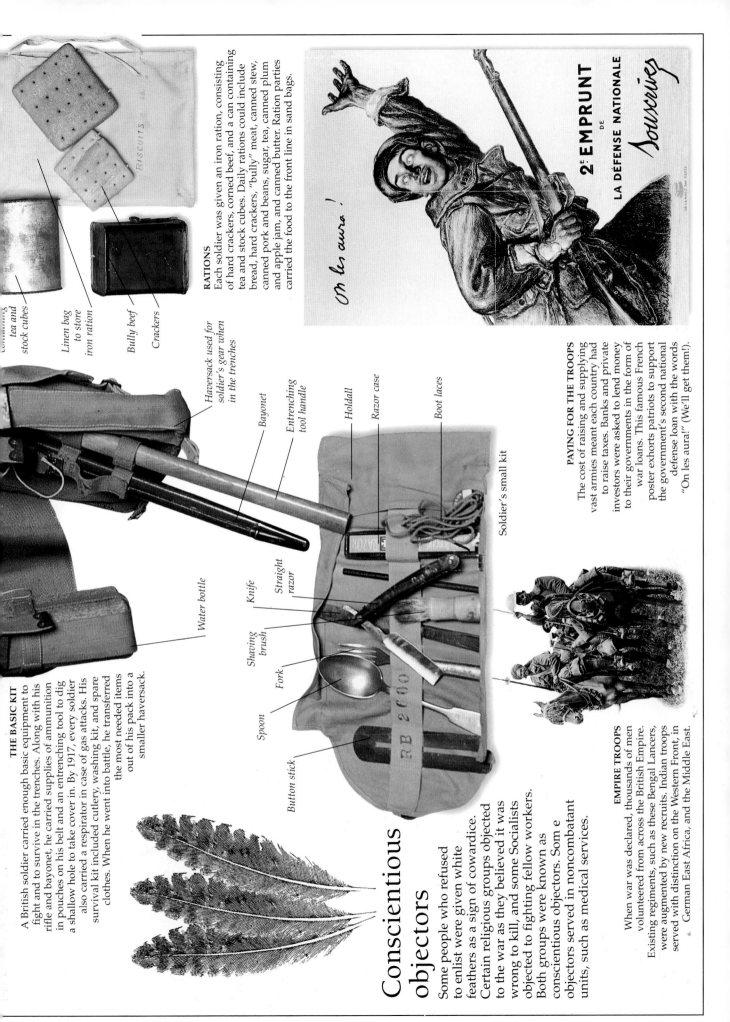

RATIONS

Each soldier was given an iron ration, consisting of hard crackers, corned beef, and a can containing tea and stock cubes. Daily rations could include bread, hard crackers, "bully" meat, canned stew, canned pork and beans, sugar, tea, canned plum and apple jam, and canned butter. Ration parties carried the food to the front line in sand bags.

containing tea and stock cubes

Linen bag to store iron ration

BISCUITS — LB.

Bully beef

Crackers

Haversack used for soldier's gear when in the trenches

Bayonet

Entrenching tool handle

Holdall

Razor case

Boot laces

Soldier's small kit

Water bottle

Knife

Straight razor

Shaving brush

Fork

Spoon

Button stick

On les aura !

2ᴱ EMPRUNT
DE
LA DÉFENSE NATIONALE
Souscrivez

DELANDRE del PARIS

PAYING FOR THE TROOPS

The cost of raising and supplying vast armies meant each country had to raise taxes. Banks and private investors were asked to lend money to their governments in the form of war loans. This famous French poster exhorts patriots to support the government's second national defense loan with the words "On les aura!" (We'll get them!).

THE BASIC KIT

A British soldier carried enough basic equipment to fight and to survive in the trenches. Along with his rifle and bayonet, he carried supplies of ammunition in pouches on his belt and an entrenching tool to dig a shallow hole to take cover in. By 1917, every soldier also carried a respirator in case of gas attacks. His survival kit included cutlery, washing kit, and spare clothes. When he went into battle, he transferred the most needed items out of his pack into a smaller haversack.

Conscientious objectors

Some people who refused to enlist were given white feathers as a sign of cowardice. Certain religious groups objected to the war as they believed it was wrong to kill, and some Socialists objected to fighting fellow workers. Both groups were known as conscientious objectors. Som e objectors served in noncombatant units, such as medical services.

EMPIRE TROOPS

When war was declared, thousands of men volunteered from across the British Empire. Existing regiments, such as these Bengal Lancers, were augmented by new recruits. Indian troops served with distinction on the Western Front, in German East Africa, and the Middle East.

15

Digging the trenches

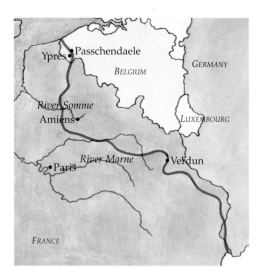

Front line of trenches

THE FRONT LINE
By December 1914, a network of trenches stretched along the Western Front from the Belgian coast in the north down through eastern France to the Swiss border, 400 miles (645 km) in the south. By 1917, it was possible in theory to walk the entire length of the front along the winding trench network.

THE FIRST TRENCHES
Early trenches were just deep furrows, which provided minimal cover from enemy fire. These troops from the 2nd Scots Guards dug this trench near Ypres in October 1914. Their generals believed that such trenches were only temporary, as the "normal" war of movement would resume in the spring.

Aᴛ ᴛʜᴇ ᴏᴜᴛʙʀᴇᴀᴋ ᴏꜰ ᴡᴀʀ, both sides on the Western Front expected to take part in massive military maneuvers over hundreds of miles of territory, and to fight fast-moving battles of advance and retreat. No one expected a static fight between two evenly matched sides. A stalemate occurred mainly because powerful long-range artillery weapons and rapid-fire machine guns made it dangerous for soldiers to fight in unprotected, open ground. The only way to survive such weapons was to dig defensive trenches.

Bla
co

ENTRENCHING TOOLS
Each soldier carried an entrenching tool. With it, the soldier could dig a scrape – a basic protective trench – if he was caught in the open by enemy fire. He could also use it to repair or improve a trench damaged by an enemy artillery bombardment.

American M1910 entrenching tool

SIGNPOSTS
Each trench was signposted to ma sure no one lost his way during attack. Nicknam frequently becan signposted name

POSITIONING THE TRENCH
Neither side had great expertise in digging trenches at the outbreak of war, but they quickly learned from their mistakes. The Germans usually built trenches where they could best observe and fire at the enemy while remaining concealed. The British and French preferred to capture as much ground as possible before digging their trenches.

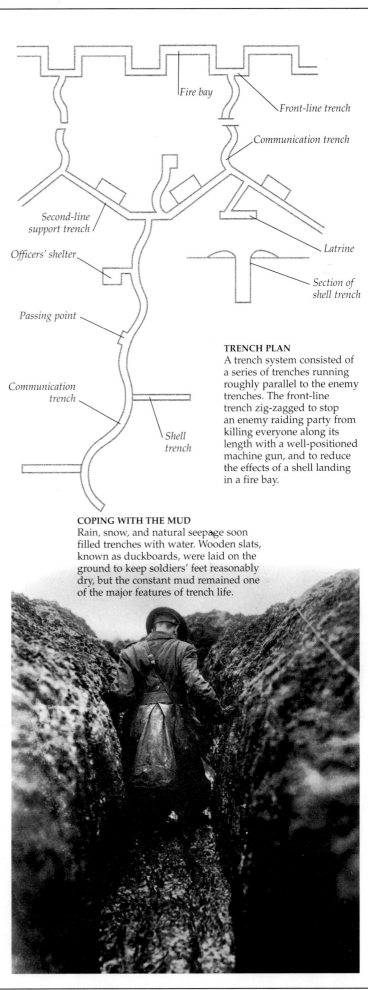

TRENCH PLAN
Fire bay

Front-line trench

Communication trench

Second-line
support trench

Latrine

Officers' shelter

Section of
shell trench

Passing point

Communication
trench

Shell
trench

...RDED UP

... of the main dangers of trench life was the possibility of
...g buried alive if the walls collapsed. By summer 1915,
...y German trenches were reinforced with wooden walls
...revent this from happening. They were also dug very
...o to help protect the men from artillery bombardments.

...ME SWEET HOME?

... Germans constructed very elaborate trenches
...ause, as far as they were concerned, this was the
...y German border. Many trenches had shuttered
...dows and even doormats to wipe muddy boots
... Allied trenches were much more basic
...ause the Allies expected to recapture
...occupied territory.

TRENCH PLAN
A trench system consisted of
a series of trenches running
roughly parallel to the enemy
trenches. The front-line
trench zig-zagged to stop
an enemy raiding party from
killing everyone along its
length with a well-positioned
machine gun, and to reduce
the effects of a shell landing
in a fire bay.

COPING WITH THE MUD
Rain, snow, and natural seepage soon
filled trenches with water. Wooden slats,
known as duckboards, were laid on the
ground to keep soldiers' feet reasonably
dry, but the constant mud remained one
of the major features of trench life.

Life in the trenches

DAYTIME IN THE TRENCHES alternated between short periods of intense fear, when the enemy fired, and longer periods of boredom. Most of the work was done at night when patrols were sent out to observe and raid enemy trenches, and to repair their own front-line parapets and other defenses. Dawn and dusk were the most likely times for an enemy attack, so all the troops "stood to," or manned the fire bays, at these times. The days were usually quiet, so the men tried to catch up on sleep while sentries watched the enemy trenches. Many soldiers used this time to write home or keep a diary of events. There were no set mealtimes on the front line, and soldiers ate as and when transportation was available to bring food to the front by carrying parties. To relieve the boredom, soldiers spent one week to 10 days on the front line, then moved into the reserve lines, and finally went to a rear area to rest. Here, they were given a bath and freshly laundered clothes before returning to the trenches.

A LITTLE SHELTER
The trenches were usually very narrow and often expo to the weather. The Canadian soldiers in this trench h built a makeshift canopy to shelter under. The sides ar made of sandbags piled on top of each other.

Soldier removing mud from ammunition pouch with a piece of cloth

A RELAXING READ?
This re-creation from London's Imperial War Museum shows a soldier reading. While there was plenty of time for the soldiers to read during the day, they were often interrupted by rats scurrying past their feet and itching lice in their clothes.

NEAT AND CLEAN
The cleaning of gear and the waterproofing of boots was as much a part of life in the trenches as it was in the barracks back home. These Belgian soldiers cleaning their rifles knew that such tasks were essential to maintaining combat efficiency.

OFFICERS' DUGOUT
This re-creation in London's Imperial War Museum of an officers' dugout on the Somme in the fall of 1916 shows the cramped conditions people endured in the trenches. The officer on the telephone is calling in artillery support for an imminent trench raid, while his weary comrade is asleep behind him on a camp bed. Official notices, photographs, and postcards from home are tacked around the walls.

The Menin Road (1918) by Paul Nash

French author Henri Barbusse (1873–1935) wrote of life in the trenches, denouncing the war, in his novel *Le Feu (Under Fire)* of 1916.

Poem and self-portrait by the British poet and artist Isaac Rosenberg (1890–1918)

Artists and poets

Some soldiers used their spare time in the trenches to write poems or make sketches. A huge number wrote long letters home or kept a diary. After the war, many of these writings were published. Literary records of trench life made fascinating and shocking reading. In 1916, the British government began to send official war artists, such as Paul Nash (1889–1946), to the front to record the war in paint.

Paints and brushes belonging to the British artist Paul Nash

CAVE MEN
Ordinary soldiers – such as these members of the British Border Regiment at Thiepval Wood on the Somme in 1916 – spent their time off duty in "funk holes," holes carved out of the side of the trench, or under waterproof sheets. Unlike the Germans, the British did not intend to stay in the trenches too long, so did not want the soldiers to make themselves comfortable.

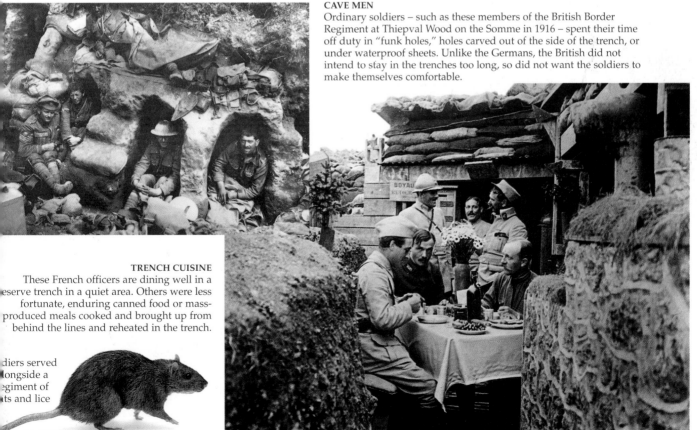

TRENCH CUISINE
These French officers are dining well in a reserve trench in a quiet area. Others were less fortunate, enduring canned food or mass-produced meals cooked and brought up from behind the lines and reheated in the trench.

Soldiers served alongside a regiment of rats and lice

Ready to fight

IT'S EASY TO imagine that most of the action on the Western Front took place when soldiers left their trenches and fought each other in open ground, no-man's land, between the two opposing front lines. In reality, such events were far rarer than the constant battle between soldiers in their facing lines of trenches. Both armies took every opportunity to take shots at anyone foolish or unfortunate enough to be visible to the other side. Even soldiers trying to rescue wounded comrades from no-man's land or retrieve bodies caught on the barbed-wire fences were considered fair targets. Raiding parties from one front line to the other added to the danger. This relentless war of attrition kept every soldier on full alert, and meant that a watch had to be kept on the enemy lines every hour of the day.

PREPARE TO FIRE
These German troops on the Marne in 191[?] are firing through custom-built gun holes. This enabled them to view and fire at the enemy without putting their heads above [the] parapet and exposing themselves to enem[y] fire. Later on in the war, sandbags replace[d] the earthen ramparts. On their backs, the troops carry leather knapsacks with rolled greatcoats and tent cloths on top.

IN CLOSE QUARTERS
Soldiers were armed with a range of close-combat weapons when they went on raiding parties in case they needed to kill an enemy. The enemy could be killed silently so that the raiding soldiers did not draw attention to themselves. The weapons were rarely used.

WRITING HOME
Canon Cyril Lomax served in France in 1916–17 as a chaplain to the 8th Battalion Durham Light Infantry. As a noncombatant, he had time to describe in illustrated letters home the horrors he encountered. The armies of both sides had chaplains and other clergy at the front.

French trench knife

German stick grenade

German club

German timed and fused ball grenade

British Mills bomb

Last time over the bags was rather terrible. The f[?] who managed to pull themselves out of the waist-deep m[ud] had to stand on the top & pull others who were stuck out [of the] trenches. Imagine doing that with machine guns hard[?] work, to say nothing of snipers. One man I know of [?] drowned in the mud. Another was only extricated by [?] men. Naturally no supports or rations could come up[?] after gaining their objectives in some cases, in others [they were] mown down at once they had to retire. I have had to make this trench too wide

WALKING WOUNDED

This re-creation in London's
Imperial War Museum shows a
wounded German prisoner
being escorted by a medical
orderly from the front line back
through the trench system to a
regimental aid post. Many,
however, were not so fortunate.
A soldier wounded in no-man's
land would be left until it was
safe to bring him back to his
trench, usually at night. Many
soldiers risked their lives to
retrieve wounded comrades.
Sadly, some soldiers died
because they could not be
reached soon enough.

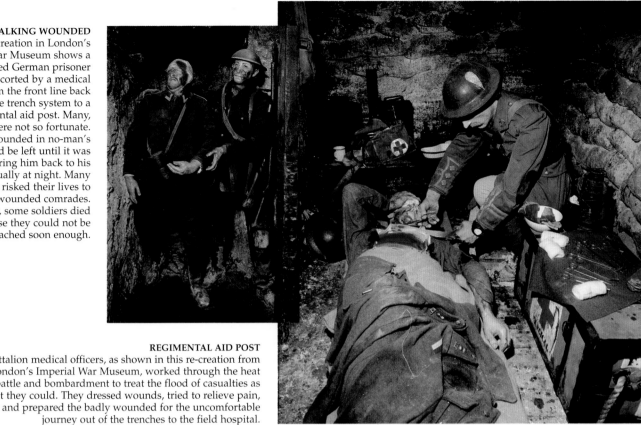

REGIMENTAL AID POST

Battalion medical officers, as shown in this re-creation from
London's Imperial War Museum, worked through the heat
of battle and bombardment to treat the flood of casualties as
best they could. They dressed wounds, tried to relieve pain,
and prepared the badly wounded for the uncomfortable
journey out of the trenches to the field hospital.

of bullet

SAVED BY A BOOK

The soldier carrying this book was lucky. By
the time the bullet had passed through the
pages, its passage was slowed enough to
minimise the injury it caused.

*The German that
I shot was a fine
looking man ... I did
feel sorry, but it
was my life or his"*

BRITISH SOLDIER JACK SWEENEY,
NOVEMBER 21, 1916

ALWAYS IN ACTION

This photograph of Bulgarian soldiers
was taken in 1915. It shows that
soldiers could never let their guard
down while in a trench. A
permanent look out must be
kept, and guns always primed
and ready in case the enemy
mounted a sudden attack. The
soldiers had to eat in
shifts to ensure
constant
readiness for
battle.

Communication and supplies

FIELD TELEPHONE
Telephones were the main communication method between the front line and headquarters. They relayed voice and Morse code messages.

Communicating with and supplying front-line troops is the biggest problem faced by every army. On the Western Front, this problem was particularly acute because of the length of the front line and the large number of soldiers fighting along it. In mid-1917, for example, the British army required 500,000 shells a day, and million-shell days were not uncommon. To supply such vast and hungry armies, both sides devoted great attention to lines of communication. The main form of transportation remained the horse, but increasing use was made of mechanized vehicles. Germany made great use of railroads to move men and supplies to the front. Both sides set up elaborate supply systems to ensure that front-line troops never ran out of munitions or food. Front-line troops also kept in close touch with headquarters and other units by telephone and wireless.

GETTING IN TOUCH
Teams of engineers – such as this German group – were trained to set up, maintain, a operate telephones in the field. This allow closer and more regular contact between t front line and HQ than in previous wars.

British night signal

MISSILE MESSAGES
Enemy fire often cut telephone lines, so both sides used shells to carry written messages. Flares on the shells lit up to signal their arrival. Signal grenades and rockets were also widely used to convey prearranged messages to front-line troops.

Canvas top secured with ropes

Message rolled up in base

German message shell

French army pigeon handler's badge

LOAD NOT TO
EXCEED 3 TONS

WD

POSTAL PIGEON
Carrier pigeons were often used to carry messages to and from the front line where telephone lines did not exist. But the noise and confusion of the front meant that the birds easily became bewildered and flew off in the wrong direction. Germany used "war dogs" specially trained to carry messages in containers on their collars.

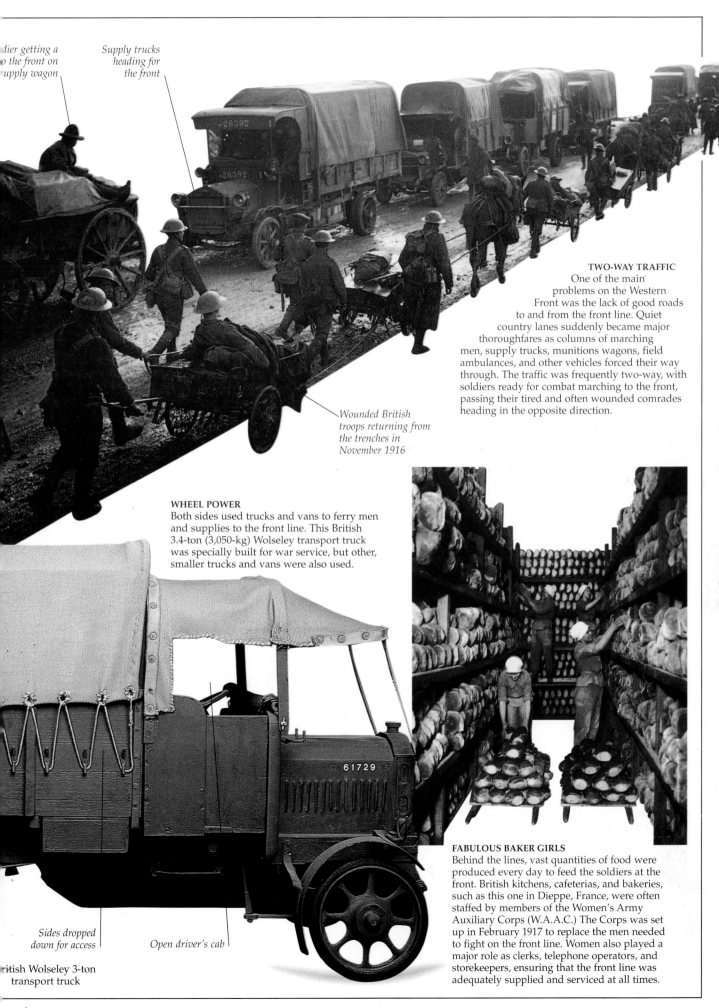

...dier getting a
...o the front on
...upply wagon

Supply trucks
heading for
the front

TWO-WAY TRAFFIC
One of the main
problems on the Western
Front was the lack of good roads
to and from the front line. Quiet
country lanes suddenly became major
thoroughfares as columns of marching
men, supply trucks, munitions wagons, field
ambulances, and other vehicles forced their way
through. The traffic was frequently two-way, with
soldiers ready for combat marching to the front,
passing their tired and often wounded comrades
heading in the opposite direction.

Wounded British
troops returning from
the trenches in
November 1916

WHEEL POWER
Both sides used trucks and vans to ferry men
and supplies to the front line. This British
3.4-ton (3,050-kg) Wolseley transport truck
was specially built for war service, but other,
smaller trucks and vans were also used.

61729

Sides dropped
down for access

Open driver's cab

...ritish Wolseley 3-ton
transport truck

FABULOUS BAKER GIRLS
Behind the lines, vast quantities of food were
produced every day to feed the soldiers at the
front. British kitchens, cafeterias, and bakeries,
such as this one in Dieppe, France, were often
staffed by members of the Women's Army
Auxiliary Corps (W.A.A.C.) The Corps was set
up in February 1917 to replace the men needed
to fight on the front line. Women also played a
major role as clerks, telephone operators, and
storekeepers, ensuring that the front line was
adequately supplied and serviced at all times.

Observation and patrol

GATHERING INTELLIGENCE ABOUT the enemy is of great importance during war, because that information can be used to mount a successful attack or repel an enemy advance. Interrogating prisoners was a very successful method of gathering information. Additionally, along the Western Front, both sides were ingenious in devising new methods to gather intelligence. Nighttime patrols probed the strengths and weaknesses of enemy lines. This was hazardous work, as it meant crossing rows of barbed-wire entanglements and perhaps disturbing an unexploded shell or attracting enemy gunfire. Observation turrets and periscopes were also used. Aircraft became increasingly popular since they could fly virtually unhindered over the enemy, observe their trenches and gun emplacements, and photograph the front line. This information could then be used to produce maps of the enemy lines.

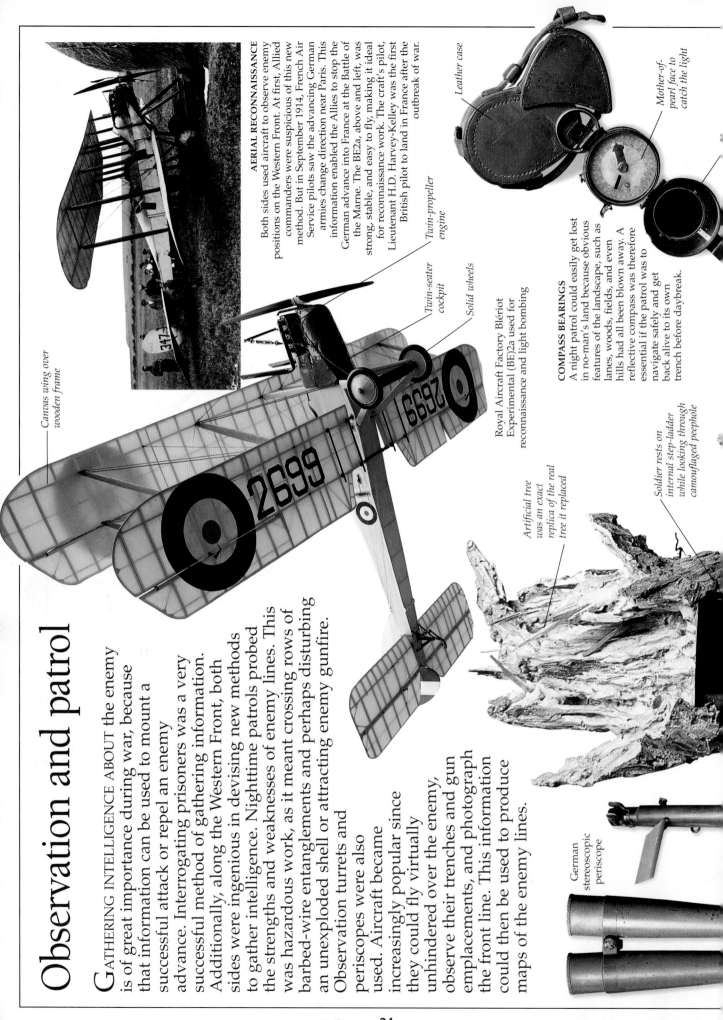

AERIAL RECONNAISSANCE
Both sides used aircraft to observe enemy positions on the Western Front. At first, Allied commanders were suspicious of this new method. But in September 1914, French Air Service pilots saw the advancing German armies change direction near Paris. This information enabled the Allies to stop the German advance into France at the Battle of the Marne. The BE2a, above and left, was strong, stable, and easy to fly, making it ideal for reconnaissance work. The craft's pilot, Lieutenant H.D. Harvey-Kelley was the first British pilot to land in France after the outbreak of war.

Twin-propeller engine

Twin-seater cockpit

Solid wheels

Canvas wing over wooden frame

Royal Aircraft Factory Blériot Experimental (BE)2a used for reconnaissance and light bombing

Leather case

Mother-of-pearl face to catch the light

COMPASS BEARINGS
A night patrol could easily get lost in no-man's land because obvious features of the landscape, such as lanes, woods, fields, and even hills had all been blown away. A reflective compass was therefore essential if the patrol was to navigate safely and get back alive to its own trench before daybreak.

Artificial tree was an exact replica of the real tree it replaced

Soldier rests on internal step-ladder while looking through camouflaged peephole

German stereoscopic periscope

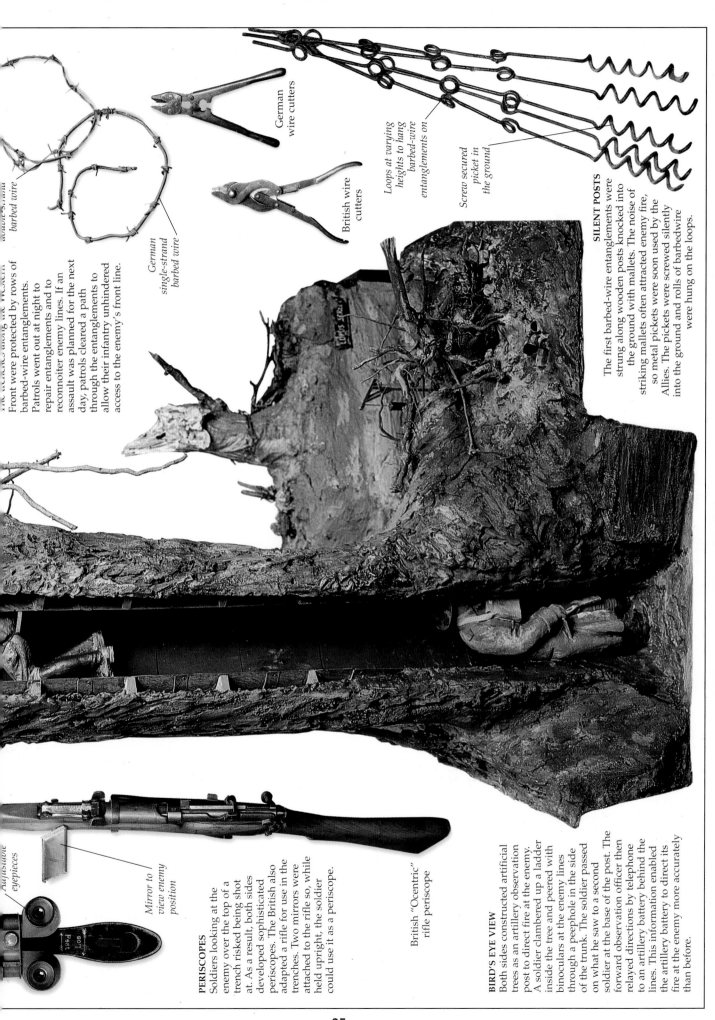

barbed wire

...along the Western Front were protected by rows of barbed-wire entanglements. Patrols went out at night to repair entanglements and to reconnoiter enemy lines. If an assault was planned for the next day, patrols cleared a path through the entanglements to allow their infantry unhindered access to the enemy's front line.

German single-strand barbed wire

German wire cutters

British wire cutters

Loops at varying heights to hang barbed-wire entanglements on

Screw secured picket in the ground

SILENT POSTS

The first barbed-wire entanglements were strung along wooden posts knocked into the ground with mallets. The noise of striking mallets often attracted enemy fire, so metal pickets were soon used by the Allies. The pickets were screwed silently into the ground and rolls of barbedwire were hung on the loops.

Adjustable eyepieces

Mirror to view enemy position

PERISCOPES

Soldiers looking at the enemy over the top of a trench risked being shot at. As a result, both sides developed sophisticated periscopes. The British also adapted a rifle for use in the trenches. Two mirrors were attached to the rifle so, while held upright, the soldier could use it as a periscope.

British "Ocentric" rifle periscope

BIRD'S EYE VIEW

Both sides constructed artificial trees as an artillery observation post to direct fire at the enemy. A soldier clambered up a ladder inside the tree and peered with binoculars at the enemy lines through a peephole in the side of the trunk. The soldier passed on what he saw to a second soldier at the base of the post. The forward observation officer then relayed directions by telephone to an artillery battery behind the lines. This information enabled the artillery battery to direct its fire at the enemy more accurately than before.

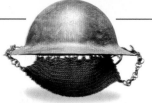

BEWARE!
Soldiers at the front needed constant reminders to keep their heads down as they were so used to shells flying past. Warning signs were common.

Bombardment

ARTILLERY DOMINATED the battlefields of World War I. A well-aimed bombardment could destroy enemy trenches, and knock out artillery batteries and communication lines. It could also help break up an infantry attack. But as defensive positions strengthened, artillery bombardments became longer and more intense. New tactics were required to break down enemy lines. The most effective was the creeping barrage, which rained down a moving curtain of heavy and insistent fire just ahead of attacking infantry.

Helmet

Visor for extra protection

GERMAN ARMOR
In January 1916 the German army replac[ed] its distinctive spiked *Pickelhaube* with a rounded steel helme[t]. Body armor was firs[t] issued in 1916 to machine gunners.

Breastplate

Articulated plates to cover lower body

HIDING THE GUN
Two main types of artillery were used during the war – light field artillery, pulled by horses, and heavier guns, such as howitzers, moved by tractor and set up on reinforced beds. Once in place, artillery pieces were camouflaged to stop the enemy from destroying them.

British 8-in (20-cm) Mark V howitzer

SHELL POWER
The huge number of shells needed to maintain a constant artillery barrage against the enemy can be seen in this photograph of a British shell dump behind the Western Front.

The devasting impact of artillery
fire can be seen in this dramatic
picture of a British tank hit by a
shell and bursting into flames.
To its right, another tank breaks
through the barbed wire. It
was unusual for moving targets,
such as tanks, to be hit, and most
artillery fire was used to soften up
the enemy lines before an attack.

ADING A HOWITZER

rge pieces of artillery required a team
experienced gunners to load and
e them. This British 15-in (38-cm)
witzer was used on the Menin
ad near Ypres, Belgium, in
tober 1917. The huge shell
the left of the picture
oo large and
avy to lift, so is
ng winched
o position.

British 13-pounder
(5.9-kg) high-
explosive shell

French
75-mm
(2.9-in)
shrapnel
shell

*Fired from
a howitzer*

British 4.5 in-
(11.4-cm) high-
explosive shell

German 15-cm (5.9-in)
shrapnel shell

CLASSIFYING SHELLS

Shells were classified by weight or diameter. High-explosive
shells exploded on impact. Antipersonnel shrapnel shells
exploded in flight and were designed to kill or maim.

Over the top

ONCE THE ARTILLERY bombardment had pounded the enemy's defenses, the infantry climbed out of the trenches and advanced toward enemy lines. The advance was very dangerous. Artillery bombardments rarely knocked out every enemy defense. Often, many gun emplacements and barbed-wire fences were still intact. Gaps in the defensive line were filled by highly mobile machine gunners. Against them, a soldier armed with only a rifle and bayonet and laden with heavy equipment was an easy target. On the first day of the Battle of the Somme in July 1916, German machine-gun fire accounted for two British soldiers killed or injured along each three feet (meter) of the 16-mile (28-km) front.

LEAVING THE TREN
The most frightening mom for a soldier was scrambling a ladder out of his trench into no-man's-land. men knew the hor that awaited th

Steel water jacket to cool gun barrel

German MG '08 Maxim machine gun

Disc is part of the flash hider assembly, making the gun harder to spot

Trench mounting

IN ACTION
This German machine-gun crew is protecting the flank (side) of an advancing infantry troop on the Western Front. The reliability and firepower of machine guns made them effective weapons. Also, their small size and maneuverability made them difficult for the enemy to destroy.

British .303-in (7.7-mm) Maxim Mark 3 medium machine gun

Water-cooled barrel

QUICK FIRING
Machine guns fired up to 600 bullets a minute. Ammunition was put into a fabric or metal-link belt, or in a metal tray fed into the gun automatically. The gun barrel was surrounded with a cold-water jacket to cool it.

Tripod mounting

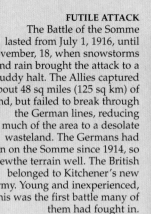

FUTILE ATTACK
The Battle of the Somme lasted from July 1, 1916, until November, 18, when snowstorms and rain brought the attack to a muddy halt. The Allies captured about 48 sq miles (125 sq km) of land, but failed to break through the German lines, reducing much of the area to a desolate wasteland. The Germans had been on the Somme since 1914, so knew the terrain well. The British belonged to Kitchener's new army. Young and inexperienced, this was the first battle many of them had fought in.

> *"The sunken road ... (was) ... filled with pieces of uniform, weapons, and dead bodies."*
>
> LIEUTENANT ERNST JUNGER,
> GERMAN SOLDIER,
> THE SOMME, 1916

First day on the Somme

The Allies planned to break through the German lines north of the Somme River, France, in 1916. On June, 24 the British began a six-day artillery bombardment on German lines, but the Germans retreated into deep bunkers and were largely unharmed. As the British infantry advanced at 7:30 am on July, 1 German machine gunners emerged from their bunkers and opened fire. Believing the artillery bombardment had destroyed German lines, the infantry marched in long, slow waves toward the enemy who literally mowed them down.

TENDING THE WOUNDED
The cramped conditions in a trench can be seen in this picture of an army medical officer tending a wounded soldier at Thiepval near the Somme in September 1916. Movement along a trench was often difficult and slow.

Below: Soldiers of the 103rd (Tyneside Irish) Brigade attack La Boisselle on the first day of the Somme

Casualty

No one knows how many soldiers were wounded in the war, but a possible figure is 21 million. Caring for casualties was a major military operation. They were first treated at regimental aid posts in the trenches. Then, they were taken to casualty clearing stations behind the front line. Here, they received proper medical attention and basic surgery, if required, before being transported to base hospitals still farther from the front. Soldiers with severe injuries went home to recover in convalescent hospitals. Over 78% of British soldiers on the Western Front returned to active service. Sickness was a major cause of casualty – in some areas, over 50% of deaths were due to disease.

LUCKY MAN
Despite a fragment from a shell piercing his helmet, this soldier escaped with only a minor head wound. Many soldiers were not so fortunate, receiving severe injuries that stayed with them for life – if they survived at all.

Invento
listing
content
where t
them in
pouch

Bottles
liquid
antisep
and pai
killers

THE GERMAN KIT
German *Sanitätsmanschaften* (medical orderlies) carried two first-aid pouches on their belts. The pouch on the right (above) contained basic antiseptics, painkillers, and other treatments, while the pouch on the left contained dressings and triangular bandages.

TRENCH AID
Injured soldiers had their wounds dressed by medical orderlies in the trenches where they fell. They were then transferred to the regimental aid post, where their injuries could be assessed.

Strip of lace curtain

German bandages

RECYCLED BANDAGES
Following the naval blockade by Britain, Germany ran out of cotton and linen. Wood fiber, paper, and lace curtains were used to make bandages instead.

Text callouts on the surgical instrument image:

...ceps and ...ps held ...rely in a ...al tray

...er tray ...tains saws ...knives for ...utation

TOOLS OF THE TRADE
Army doctors carried a standard set of
surgical instruments, as in this set issued by
the Indian army. Their skills were in great
demand, as they faced a wide variety of
injuries from bullets and shell fragments
that required immediate attention.

THE FIELD HOSPITAL
Farmhouses, ruined factories, and even bombed-out churches, such as this
one in Meuse, France, were used as casualty clearing stations to treat the
wounded. Care was basic, and many were left to help themselves.

Shellshock

Shellshock is the collective name that was used to describe
concussion, emotional shock, nervous exhaustion, and other similar
ailments. Shellshock was not known before World War I, but trench
warfare was so horrific that many soldiers developed shellshock
during this war. Most of them eventually recovered, but some
suffered nightmares and other symptoms for the rest of their
lives. The illness caused a lot of controversy, and in 1922, the
British War Office Committee said that shellshock did not
exist and that it was a collection of already known illnesses.

_A medical
orderly helps a
wounded soldier
away from the
trenches_

_Bunks for the
injured to lie on_

AMBULANCE
The British Royal Army
Medical Corps, like its
German counterpart, had a
fleet of field ambulances to
carry the wounded to the
hospital. Many of these
ambulances were staffed
by volunteers, often
women, and those from
noncombatant countries
such as the US.

_Red Cross symbol to
signify non-
combatant status of
the ambulance_

Women at war

WHEN THE MEN went off to fight, the women were called upon to take their place on the homefront. Many women were already working, but their role was restricted to domestic labor, nursing, teaching, agricultural work on the family farm, and a few other jobs considered suitable for women. Now they went to work in factories, drove trucks and ambulances, and did almost everything that only men had done before. Many working women left their low-paid, low-status jobs for higher-paid work in munitions and other industries, achieving a new status in the eyes of society. Such gains, however, were short-lived, as most women returned to the home when the war ended.

FRONT-LINE ADVENTURE
For some women, the war was a big adventure. English nurse Elsie Knocker (above) went to Belgium in 1914 where she was joined by Scottish Mairi Chisholm. The women set up a dressing station in Pervyse, Belgium, and dressed the wounded until both were gassed in 1918. They were almost the only women on the front line. The two became known as the Women of Pervyse and were awarded the Order of Leopold by Belgian King Albert, and the British Military Medal. Elsie later married a Belgian officer, Baron de T'Sercl...

ARMY LAUNDRY
Traditional prewar women's work, such as working in a laundry or bakery, continued during the war on a much larger scale. The French women employed at this British Army laundry in Prevent, France, in 1918 were washing and cleaning the dirty clothes of many thousands of soldiers every day.

QUEEN MARY'S AUXILIARY
Few women actually fought in the war, but many were enlisted into auxiliary armies so that men could be released to fight on the front line. They drove trucks, repaired engines, and did much of the necessary administration and supply work. In Britain, many women joined The Women's (later Queen Mary's) Army Auxiliary Corps, whose recruiting poster featured a khaki-clad woman (left) with the words "The girl behind the man behind the gun." The women remained civilians, despite their military work.

[WO]MEN'S LAND ARMY

[The] war required a huge increase in food production at home as both sides [trie]d to restrict the enemy's imports of food from abroad. In Britain, 113,000 [wo]men joined the Women's Land Army, set up in February 1917 to provide [a we]ll-paid female workforce to run the farms. Many members of the Land [Arm]y, such as this group of healthy-looking women, came from the middle [and] upper classes. They made a valuable contribution, but their numbers [wer]e insignificant compared with the millions of working-class women [alre]ady employed on the land in the rest of Europe.

[RUS]SIA'S AMAZONS

[A nu]mber of Russian women joined the "Legion of Death" to fight [for t]heir country. The first battalion from Petrograd (St. Petersburg) [disti]nguished itself by taking more than 100 German prisoners during [a Ru]ssian retreat, although many of the women died in the battle.

Letters to men at the front describing events at home

Family photographs

Lace handkerchief

SUPPORT YOUR COUNTRY

Images of "ideal" women were used to gain support for a country's war effort. This Russian poster urges people to buy war bonds (fund-raising loans to the government) by linking Russian women to the love of the motherland.

WORKING IN POVERTY

The war brought increased status and wealth to many women, but this was not the case everywhere. These Italian women worked in terrible conditions in a munitions factory. Many were very young and could not even afford shoes. This was common in factories across Italy, Germany, and Russia. The women worked long, hard hours but earned barely enough to feed their families. Strikes led by women were very common as a result.

MEMENTOS FROM HOME

Women kept in contact with their absent husbands, brothers, and sons by writing letters to them at the front. They also enclosed keepsakes of home, such as photographs or pressed flowers, to reassure the men that all was well in their absence and to remind them of home. Such letters and mementos did much to keep up the morale of homesick, and often very frightened, men.

War in the air

DOGFIGHTS
Pilots engaged in dogfights with enemy aircraft above the Western Front. Guns were mounted on top of the craft, so pilots had to fly straight at the enemy to shoot.

WHEN WAR BROKE OUT in August 1914, the history of powered flight was barely 10 years old. Aircraft had fought briefly in the Italian–Turkish war of 1911, but early aircraft development had been almost entirely for civilian use. Some military leaders could not even see how aircraft could be used in war but they soon changed their minds. The first warplanes flew as reconnaissance craft, looking down on enemy lines or helping to direct artillery fire with great precision. Enemy pilots tried to shoot them down, leading to dogfights in the sky between highly skilled and immensely brave "aces." Specialized fighter planes, such as the Sopwith Camel and the German Fokkers, were soon produced by both sides, as were sturdier craft capable of carrying bombs to drop on enemy targets.
By the end of the war, the role of military aircraft had changed from being a minor help to the ground forces into a major force in their own right.

Leather face mask

Leather balaclava

Anti-splinter glass goggles

Raised collar to keep neck warm

Pouch to keep maps in

Coat of soft, supple leather

SOPWITH CAMEL
The Sopwith F1 Camel first flew in battle in June 1917 and became the most successful Allied fighter in shooting down German aircraft. Pilots enjoyed flying the Camel because of its exceptional agility and ability to make sharp turns at high speed.

Wooden box-structure wings covered with canvas

Sheepskin-lined leather gloves to protect against frostbite

26-ft 11-in (8.2-m) wingspan

DRESSED FOR THE AIR
Pilots flew in open cockpits, so they wore soft leather coats and balaclavas, sheepskin-lined fur boots, and sheepskin-lined leather gloves to keep out the cold. Later in the war, one-piece suits of waxed cotton lined with silk and fur became common.

Sheepskin boots

Propeller to guide the bomb

BOMBS AWAY
The first bombs were literally dropped over the side of the aircraft by the pilot. Specialized bomber aircraft soon appeared, equipped with bombsights, bomb racks beneath the fuselage, and release systems operated by the pilot or another crew member.

Fins to stop bomb from spinning on its descent

Perforated casing help bomb catch on impact

Thick sole to give a good grip

British 20-lb (9.1-kg) Marten Hale bomb, containing 4.5 lb (2 kg) of explosives

British Carcass incendiary bomb

Fokker DV11

GERMAN FIGHTER
The formidable German Fokker DVII appeared in April 1918. Although slower than the Sopwith Camel, it climbed rapidly, recovered quickly from a dive, and flew well at all altitudes.

Side cutaway to show internal steel-tubing framework

BMW engine

MANEUVERS
The art of aerial warfare was unknown to pilots at the start of the war and had to be learned from scratch. This British instruction poster shows the correct method of attacking a German fighter, although theory on the ground was no substitute for actual experience in the sky.

German aircraft holds a steady course

British fighter comes up from below and behind

Wooden struts

Symbol of British Royal Flying Corps, later the Royal Air Force

N6812

Barrel could fire 1-pound shell

Rittmeister Manfred von Richthofen (Germany), center – 80 hits (1892–1918)

Pivot to change direction and angle of gun

...ptain René
...ck (France)
... – 75 hits
...894–1953)

ANTIAIRCRAFT GUNS
The first antiaircraft guns, such as this British QF 1-pounder, were actually installed on ships to fire at torpedo boats. Once adapted for high-angle shooting, they became useful anti-aircraft guns on land.

AIR ACES
To qualify as an air "ace," a pilot had to bring down at least 10 enemy aircraft. Those who did became national heroes. Baron von Richthofen – the "Red Baron" – was the highest-scoring ace of the war, shooting down 80 Allied aircraft. The British ace, Captain Albert Ball, had more decorations for bravery than any other man of his age, including the Victoria Cross; he was only 20 when he was shot down and killed in 1917.

Captain Eddie Rickenbacker (USA) – 24 ⅓ hits (1890–1973)

...tain Albert Ball
...tain) – 44 hits
...1896–1917)

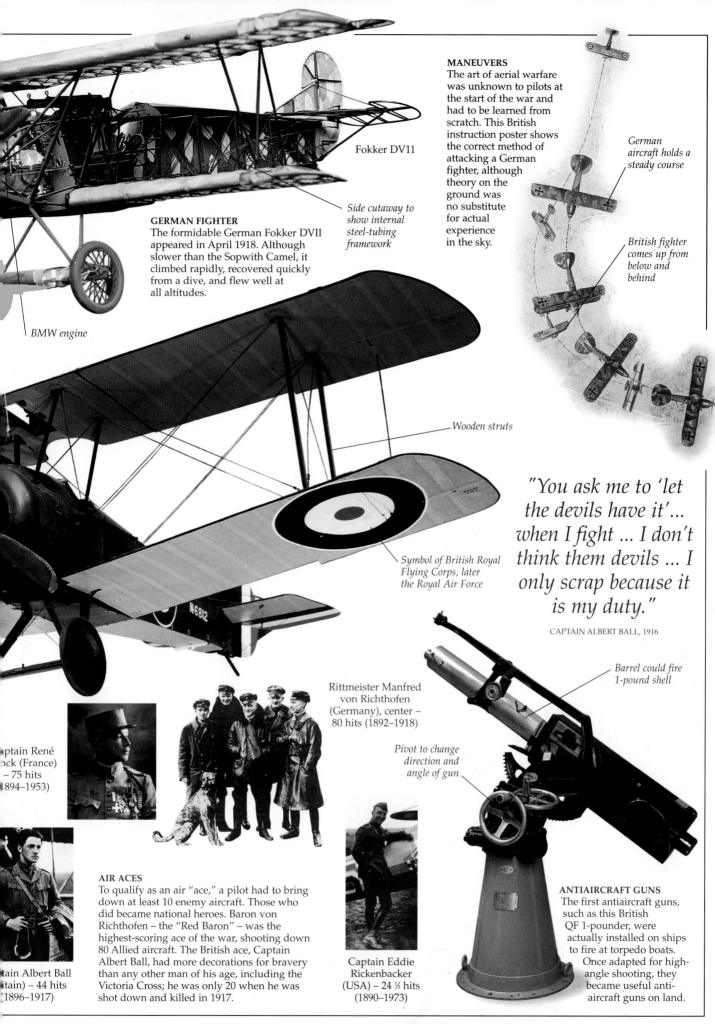

Zeppelin

I𝑁 THE SPRING OF 1915, the first German airships appeared in Britain's night sky. The sight of these huge, slow-moving machines caused enormous panic – at any moment a hail of bombs could fall from the airship. Yet in reality, airships played little part in the war. The first airship was designed by a German, Count Ferdinand von Zeppelin in 1900. Airships are often called zeppelins, but technically only those designed by him should bear the name. Early in the war, airships could fly higher than planes, so it was almost impossible to shoot them down. This made them useful for bombing raids. But soon, higher-flying aircraft and the use of incendiary (fire-making) bullets brought these aerial bombers down to earth. By 1917, most German and British airships were restricted to reconnaissance work at sea.

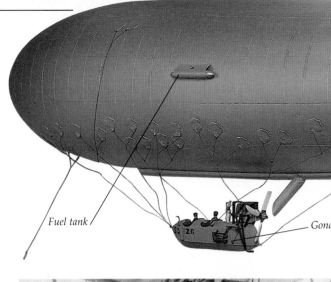

Fuel tank /   Gona

INSIDE THE GONDOLA
The crew operated the airship from the gondola – a spacious cabin below the main airship. The gondola had open sides, so the crew had little protection from the weather.

BOMBS AWAY!
Crews in the first airships had to drops their bombs, such as this incendiary bomb, over the side of the gondola by hand. Later models had automatic release mechanisms.

German incendiary bomb dropped by Zeppelin LZ38 on London, May 31, 1915

GETTING BIGGER
This L3 German airship took part in the first airship raid on Britain on the night of January 19–20, 1915, causing 20 civilian casualties. Eyewitnesses were scared by its size, but by 1918 Germany was producing ships almost three times as big.

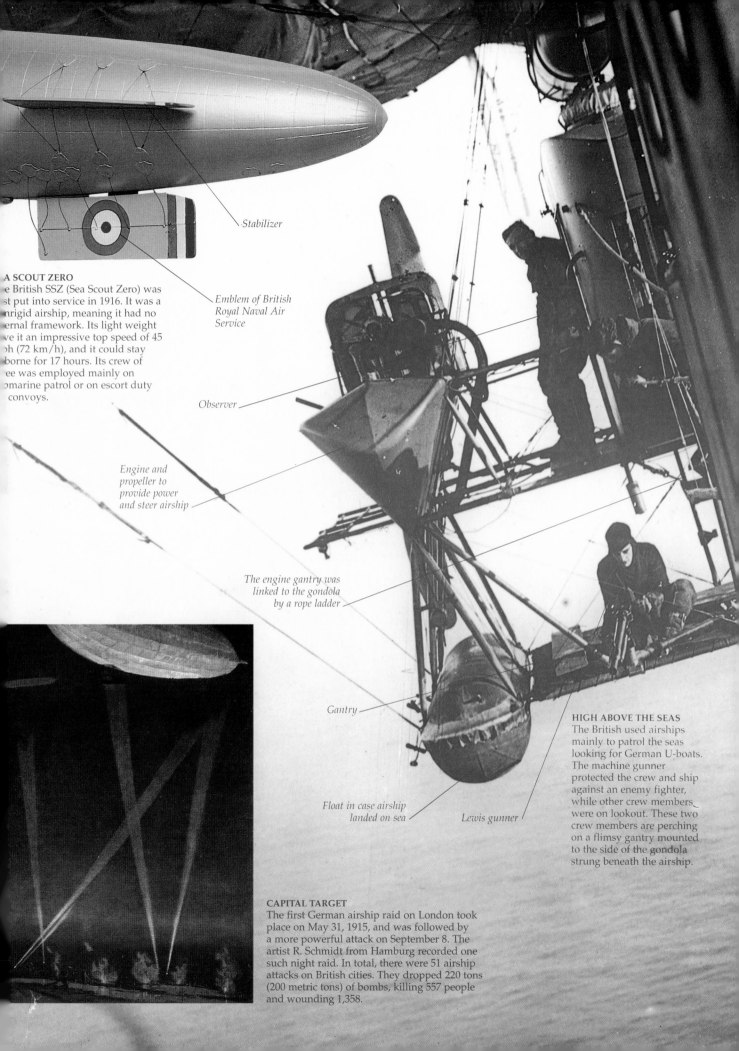

Stabilizer

Emblem of British
Royal Naval Air
Service

A SCOUT ZERO

e British SSZ (Sea Scout Zero) was
st put into service in 1916. It was a
nrigid airship, meaning it had no
ernal framework. Its light weight
ve it an impressive top speed of 45
ph (72 km/h), and it could stay
borne for 17 hours. Its crew of
ee was employed mainly on
omarine patrol or on escort duty
convoys.

Observer

Engine and
propeller to
provide power
and steer airship

The engine gantry was
linked to the gondola
by a rope ladder

Gantry

Float in case airship
landed on sea

Lewis gunner

HIGH ABOVE THE SEAS
The British used airships
mainly to patrol the seas
looking for German U-boats.
The machine gunner
protected the crew and ship
against an enemy fighter,
while other crew members
were on lookout. These two
crew members are perching
on a flimsy gantry mounted
to the side of the gondola
strung beneath the airship.

CAPITAL TARGET
The first German airship raid on London took
place on May 31, 1915, and was followed by
a more powerful attack on September 8. The
artist R. Schmidt from Hamburg recorded one
such night raid. In total, there were 51 airship
attacks on British cities. They dropped 220 tons
(200 metric tons) of bombs, killing 557 people
and wounding 1,358.

War at sea

SINCE THE LAUNCH OF Britain's *Dreadnought* battleship in 1906, Britain, Germany, and other countries had engaged in a massive naval building program. Yet the war itself was fought largely on land, and both sides avoided naval conflict. The British needed their fleet to keep the seas open for merchant ships bringing food and supplies to Britain, as well as to stop supplies from reaching Germany. Germany needed its fleet to protect itself against possible invasion. The only major sea battle – off Danish Jutland in the North Sea in 1916 – was inconclusive. The main fight took place under the sea, as German U-boats waged a damaging war against Allied merchant and troop ships in an effort to force Britain out of the war.

"I WANT YOU"
When the US entered the war in April 1917, a poster showing an attractive woman in naval uniform (above) urged volunteers to enlist.

CONSTANT THREAT
This German propaganda poster, *The U-boats are out!*, shows the threat posed to Allied shipping by the German U-boat fle

LIFE INSIDE A U-BOAT
Conditions inside a U-boat were cramped and uncomfortable. Fumes and heat from the engine and poor ventilation made the air very stuffy. The crew had to navigate the craft through minefields and avoid detection from reconnaissance aircraft in order to attack enemy ships.

Floats for landing on water

LAND AND SEA
Seaplanes are able to take off and land on both water and ground. They were use for reconnaissance and bombing work. This version of the Short 18 was the first seaplane to sink a enemy ship with a torpedo.

Observation balloon

Gun

SUCCESS AND FAILURE
German U-boats operated both und the sea and on the surface. Here, the crew is opening fire with a deck cannon to stop an enemy steamer. German U-boats sank 5,554 Allied and neutral merchant ships as well as many warships. Their own losse however, were also considerable. O of a total fleet of 372 German U-boa 178 were destroyed by Allied bomb or torpedoes.

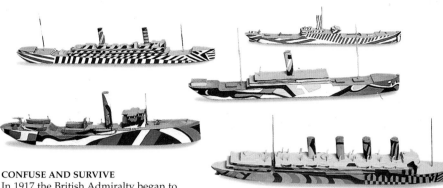

CONFUSE AND SURVIVE
In 1917 the British Admiralty began to camouflage merchant ships with strange and garish designs. These gray, black, and blue geometric patterns distorted the silhouette of the ship and made it difficult for German U-boats to determine its course and thus aim torpedoes at it with any accuracy. More than 2,700 merchant ships and 400 convoy escorts were camouflaged in this way before the war ended.

ZZLED
ring the war, many artists contributed heir country's war effort some in prising ways. The modern British nter Edward Wadsworth supervised the plication of "dazzle" camouflage to ps' hulls. He later painted a picture ove), *Dazzle ships in dry dock at Liverpool*, he finished result.

Medals awarded to Jack Cornwall

Victoria Cross (VC) British War Medal Victory Medal

BOY (1ST CLASS)
John Travers Cornwall was only 16 when he first saw action at the Battle of Jutland on May 31, 1916. He was a ship's boy (1st class) aboard HMS *Chester* and was mortally wounded early in the battle. While other crew members lay dead or injured, Cornwall stayed at his post until the end of the action. He died of his wounds on June 2, and was posthumously awarded the Victoria Cross.

THE BRITISH GRAND FLEET
The British Royal Navy was the biggest and most powerful in the world. It operated a policy known as the "two-power standard" – the combined might of the British fleet should be the equal of the two next strongest nations combined. Despite this superiority, the navy played a fairly minor role in the war compared to the army, keeping the seas free of German ships and escorting convoys of merchant ships to Britain.

— Flight deck

S FURIOUS
craft carriers first
y service during World
r I. On July 7, 1918, seven
with Camels took off from
deck of HMS *Furious* to attack
zeppelin base at Tondern in
thern Germany, destroying both
ds and the two Zeppelins inside.

TASTY GREETINGS
British army cookies were often easier to write on than to eat, as this hard-baked Christmas card from Gallipoli illustrates.

Gallipoli

In early 1915, the Allies decided to force through the strategic, but heavily fortified, Dardanelles straits and capture the Ottoman Turkish capital of Constantinople. Naval attacks on February 19, and March 18 both failed. On April 25, British, Australian, and New Zealand troops landed on the Gallipoli peninsula, while French troops staged a diversion to their south. In August, there was a second landing at Suvla Bay, also on the peninsula. Although the landings were a success, the casualty rate was high and the Allies were unable to move far from the beaches due to fierce Turkish resistance. As the months wore on, the death rate mounted. The Allies eventually withdrew in January 1916, leaving the Ottoman Empire still in control of the Dardanelles and still in the war.

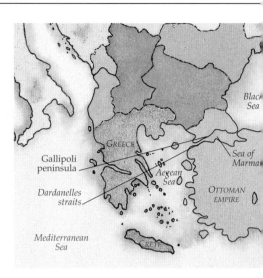

GALLIPOLI PENINSULA
The Gallipoli peninsula lies to the north of the Dardanelles, a narrow waterway connecting the Aegean Sea to the Black Sea via the Sea of Marmara. Control of this waterway would have given Britain and France a direct sea route from the Mediterranean to the Black Sea and their ally, Russia. But both sides of the waterway were controlled by Germany's ally, the Ottoman Empire.

Privately purchased medical kit used by a British officer on the front line

Hypodermic needles   *Pouch*

Scissors Scalpel   *Tweezers*

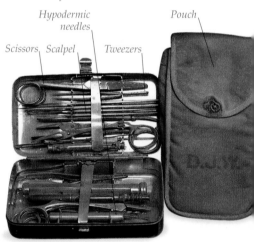

THE CASUALTY RATE
Despite the efforts of the medical staff, some of whom even carried portable surgical kits, the treatment and evacuation of casualties from Gallipoli was complicated by the enormous numbers of soldiers who were sick, as well as those who were wounded.

Jetty for boats carrying sick and wounded soldiers

THE SICK BEACH
Both sides had their food contaminated by flies carrying disease from the many corpses. Dysentery was endemic – in September 1915, 78% of the Anzac troops in the No. 1 Australian Stationary Hospital at Anzac Cove (above) were being treated for the disease.

GERMAN HELP
The Allies expected the Gallipoli peninsula to be lightly defended, but with the help of Germany, the Turks had built strong defensive positions. They dug trenches, erected barbed-wire fences, and built well-guarded artillery positions. Germany also equipped the Turks with modern pistols, rifles, and machine guns.

IMPROVISED GRENADES
The fighting at Gallipoli was often at very close range. Hand-thrown grenades were particularly effective in knocking out enemy positions. During a munitions shortage, Allied troops improvised by making grenades out of tin cans.

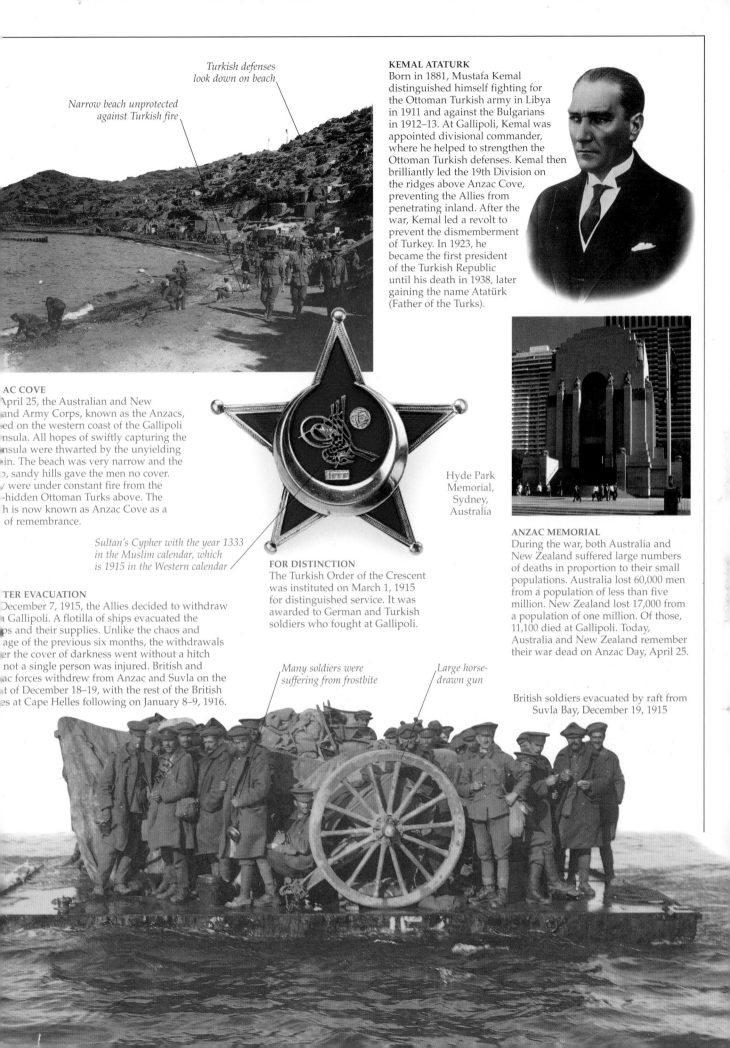

*Turkish defenses
look down on beach*

*Narrow beach unprotected
against Turkish fire*

KEMAL ATATURK
Born in 1881, Mustafa Kemal distinguished himself fighting for the Ottoman Turkish army in Libya in 1911 and against the Bulgarians in 1912–13. At Gallipoli, Kemal was appointed divisional commander, where he helped to strengthen the Ottoman Turkish defenses. Kemal then brilliantly led the 19th Division on the ridges above Anzac Cove, preventing the Allies from penetrating inland. After the war, Kemal led a revolt to prevent the dismemberment of Turkey. In 1923, he became the first president of the Turkish Republic until his death in 1938, later gaining the name Atatürk (Father of the Turks).

AC COVE
April 25, the Australian and New and Army Corps, known as the Anzacs, ed on the western coast of the Gallipoli nsula. All hopes of swiftly capturing the nsula were thwarted by the unyielding in. The beach was very narrow and the p, sandy hills gave the men no cover. y were under constant fire from the -hidden Ottoman Turks above. The h is now known as Anzac Cove as a of remembrance.

*Sultan's Cypher with the year 1333
in the Muslim calendar, which
is 1915 in the Western calendar*

TER EVACUATION
December 7, 1915, the Allies decided to withdraw Gallipoli. A flotilla of ships evacuated the ps and their supplies. Unlike the chaos and age of the previous six months, the withdrawals er the cover of darkness went without a hitch not a single person was injured. British and ac forces withdrew from Anzac and Suvla on the t of December 18–19, with the rest of the British es at Cape Helles following on January 8–9, 1916.

FOR DISTINCTION
The Turkish Order of the Crescent was instituted on March 1, 1915 for distinguished service. It was awarded to German and Turkish soldiers who fought at Gallipoli.

Hyde Park
Memorial,
Sydney,
Australia

ANZAC MEMORIAL
During the war, both Australia and New Zealand suffered large numbers of deaths in proportion to their small populations. Australia lost 60,000 men from a population of less than five million. New Zealand lost 17,000 from a population of one million. Of those, 11,100 died at Gallipoli. Today, Australia and New Zealand remember their war dead on Anzac Day, April 25.

*Many soldiers were
suffering from frostbite*

*Large horse-
drawn gun*

British soldiers evacuated by raft from
Suvla Bay, December 19, 1915

The battle of Verdun

O<small>N</small> FEBRUARY 21, 1916, Germany launched a massive attack against Verdun, a fortified French city. Verdun lay close to the German border and controlled access into eastern France. After a huge, eight-hour artillery bombardment, the German infantry advanced. The French were caught by surprise and lost control some of their main forts, but during the summer their resistance stiffened. By December, the Germans had been pushed back almost to where they started. The cost to both sides was enormous – over 400,000 French casualties and 336,831 German casualties. The German General Falkenhayn later claimed he had tried to bleed France to death. He did not succeed, and including losses at the Battle of the Somme, German casualties that year were 774,153.

BURNING WRECKAGE
On February 25, the ancient city of Verdun was evacuated. Many buildings were hit by the artillery bombardment, and even more destroyed by the fires that often raged for days. Firefighters did their best to control the blazes, but large numbers of houses had wooden frames and burned easily.

GENERAL PETAIN
General Henri-Philippe Pé[tain] took command of the Fren[ch] forces of Verdun on Febru[ary] 25, the same day as the los[s] of Fort Douaumont. He organized an effective def[ense] of the town and made sur[e] the army was properly supplied. His rallying c[ry] "Ils ne passeront pas!" (They shall not pass!) did much to raise French morale.

Exposed concrete fort wall

Machine-gun post

FORT DOUAUMONT
Verdun was protected by three rings of fortifications. Fort Douaumont, in the outer ring, was the strongest of these forts. It was built of steel and concrete and surrounded by ramparts, ditches, and rolls of barbed wire. But although the fort itself was strong, it was defended by just 56 elderly reservists. The fort fell to the Germans on February 25.

Background picture: ruined Verdun cityscape, 1916

Double-breaste[d] overcoat

Horizon-blue uniform

Haversack

LE POILU
The French slang for an infantry soldier was *le po[ilu]* or "hairy one." *Les poilus* bore the brunt of the German attack, enduring the muddy, cold, and we[t] conditions and suffering appalling injuries from shellfire and poison gas

Lebel rifle

Steel helmet

Thick boots with puttees wrapped around the legs

AT CLOSE QUARTERS
Fighting at Verdun was particularly fierce, as both sides repeatedly attacked and counterattacked the same forts and strategic areas around the city. Advancing attackers were assaulted by hails of machine-gun fire from the enemy within the forts. The open ground was so exposed that it was impossible to retrieve the dead, and the corpses were left to rot in the ground. The forts were also riddled with underground tunnels where both sides engaged in vicious hand-to-hand combat. Many dramatic films have been made about the war, and this photograph comes from one such film.

"What a bloodbath, what horrid images, what a slaughter. I just cannot find the words to express my feelings. Hell cannot be this dreadful."

ALBERT JOUBAIRE
FRENCH SOLDIER, VERDUN, 1916

ROUNDING VILLAGES
village of Ornes was one of many ch villages attacked and captured ng the German advance on un. The devastation was so great this village, along with eight rs, was not rebuilt after the war, s still marked on maps as a sign membrance.

Laurel-leaf wreath

Oak-leaf wreath

Head of Marianne, symbol of France

LEGION D'HONNEUR
In recognition of the suffering perienced by Verdun's population, French president Raymond Poincaré rded the city the *Légion d'Honneur*. The honor is usually presented to men and men, military and civilian, for bravery.

THE MUDDY INFERNO
The countryside around Verdun is wooded and hilly, with many streams running down to the Meuse River. Heavy rainfall and constant artillery bombardment turned this landscape into a desolate mudbath, where the bodies of the dead lay half-buried in shell craters and men were forced to eat and sleep within inches of their fallen comrades. This photograph shows the "Ravine de la Mort," the Ravine of the Dead.

Gas attack

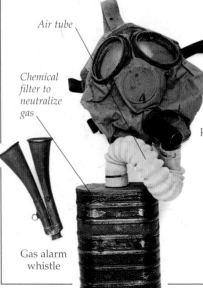

British "Hypo" helmet

ON THE AFTERNOON of April 22, 1915, French-Algerian troops near the Belgian town of Ypres noticed a greenish-yellow cloud moving toward them from the German front. The cloud was chlorine gas. This was the first time poison gas had been used effectively in war. As it reached the Allied line, many soldiers panicked, since they had no protection against its choking effects. Over the next three years, both sides used gas – the Germans released about 68,000 tons, the British and French 51,000 tons. The first gas clouds were released from canisters and blown by the wind toward the enemy, but this caused problems if the wind changed and blew the gas in the wrong direction. More effective were gas-filled shells, which could be targeted at enemy lines. In total, 1,200,000 soldiers on both sides were gassed, of whom 91,198 died terrible deaths.

EARLY WARNING
The first anti-gas masks were crude and often ineffectual, as these instructional drawings from a British training school show. Basic goggles protected the eyes, while mouthpads made of flannel or other absorbent materials were worn over the mouth. Chemicals soaked into the pads neutralized the gas.

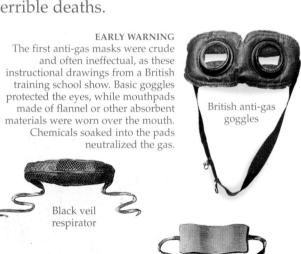

British anti-gas goggles

Black veil respirator

Flannel respirator

Air tube

Chemical filter to neutralize gas

Gas alarm whistle

ALL-IN-ONE
By the middle of the war, both sides wore fully protective helmets, which consisted of face masks, goggles, and respirators. These protected the eyes, nose, and throat from the potentially lethal effects of gas.

GASSED!
The full horror of being blinded by gas is caught in *Gassed*, a painting from real life by the American artist John Singer Sargent. Led by their sighted colleagues, the blinded soldiers are slowly shuffling toward a dressing station near Arras in northern France in August 1918.

Lachrymatory | Phosgene & Diphosgene | Diphosgene & Sneezing Oil | Diphosgene | Mustard Oil

GAS SHELLS

Gas shells contained liquid gas, which evaporated on impact. Gases caused a range of injuries depending on their type. Gases such as chlorine, diphosgene, and phosgene caused severe breathing difficulties, while benzyl bromide caused the eyes to water. Dichlorethylsulphide burned and blistered the skin, caused temporary blindness and, if inhaled, flooded the lungs and led to death from pneumonia.

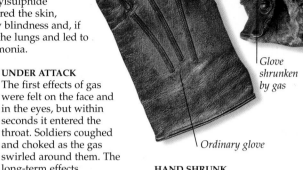

Glove shrunken by gas

Ordinary glove

HAND SHRUNK

When exposed to some kinds of gas, a glove like the one above will shrink to the size of the glove above, right. This is what happens to a person's lungs when exposed to the same gas.

UNDER ATTACK

The first effects of gas were felt on the face and in the eyes, but within seconds it entered the throat. Soldiers coughed and choked as the gas swirled around them. The long-term effects depended on the type of gas used – some soldiers died very quickly, others were blinded for life or suffered awful skin blisters, while some died a lingering death as their lungs collapsed and filled with liquid. The only protection was to wear combined goggles and respirator. Major Tracy Evert photographed these American soldiers in 1918. They are posing to illustrate the ill effects of forgetting their gas masks. The photograph was used when training new recruits.

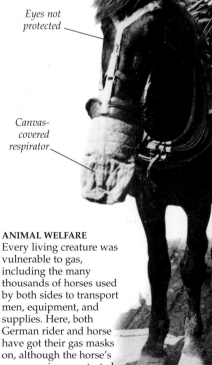

German gas mask

Eyes not protected

Canvas-covered respirator

ANIMAL WELFARE

Every living creature was vulnerable to gas, including the many thousands of horses used by both sides to transport men, equipment, and supplies. Here, both German rider and horse have got their gas masks on, although the horse's eyes remain unprotected and vulnerable.

The Eastern Front

WHEN PEOPLE TODAY think of World War I, they picture the fighting in the trenches along the Western Front. But on the other side of Europe, a very different war took place, between Germany and Austria-Hungary on one side and Russia on the other. This war was much more fluid, with great armies marching backward and forward across many hundreds of miles. Both the Austro-Hungarian and Russian armies were badly led and poorly equipped, and both suffered huge losses. In 1915 alone, the Russians lost two million men, of whom one million were taken prisoner. The German army, ably led by General Hindenburg, was far more effective. By the end of 1916, despite some Russian successes, the Germans were in full control of the entire Eastern Front. The Russians were greatly demoralized and this led, in part, to the Russian Revolution the following year, 1917.

TANNENBERG, 1914
In August 1914, Russia's First and Second armies invaded East Prussia, Germany. The Russians did not disguise their messages in code, so the Germans knew what to expect. The Second Army was soon surrounded at Tannenberg and was forced to surrender on August 31, with the loss of 150,000 men and all of its artillery (above).

MASURIAN LAKES, 1914
In September 1914, the Russian First Ar was by the Masurian Lakes in East Pru It was in danger of being surrounded a the Second Army had been the previou month at Tannenberg. German troops d trenches and other defenses (above) an attacked the Russians, who soon withd sustaining more than 100,000 casualties the end of September, the Russian threa Germany was over.

INITIAL SUCCESS
During 1914, the Russian army conquered Austria-Hungary's eastern province of Galicia, inflicting huge defeats on the Austro-Hungarian army. But, in 1915, German reinforcements (above) pushed the Russians back into their own country.

The Italian Front

On May 23, 1915, Italy joined the war on the side of the Allies and prepared to invade its hostile neighbor, Austria-Hungary. Fighting took place on two fronts – north and east. Italy fought against the Italian-speaking Trentino region of Austria-Hungary to the north, and along the Isonzo River to the east. The Italian army was ill-prepared and underequipped for the war, and was unable to break through the Austrian defenses until its final success at the Battle of Vittorio-Veneto in October 1918.

THE ISONZO
The Isonzo River formed a natural boundary between the mountains of Austria-Hungary and the plains of northern Italy. Between June 1915 and August 1917, the two sides fought 11 inconclusive battles along the river before the Austrians, with German support, achieved a decisive victory at Caporetto in December 1917.

ITALIAN ALPINISTS
All but 20 miles (32 km) of the 400-mile (640-km) Italian frontier with Austria-Hungary lay in the Italian Alps. Both sides used trained alpine troops to fight in mountainous terrain. Every mountain peak became a potential observation post or gun emplacement.

WILLING TO FIGHT
he end of 1916, many Russian soldiers were refusing to
. They were badly treated, ill-equipped, poorly led,
starving. They saw little reason to risk their lives in a
they did not believe in. Officers had to threaten their
ps to make them fight, and mutinies were common,
ugh many thousands simply deserted and went home.

Russian troops marching to defend the newly captured city of Przemysl in Austrian Galicia

War in the desert

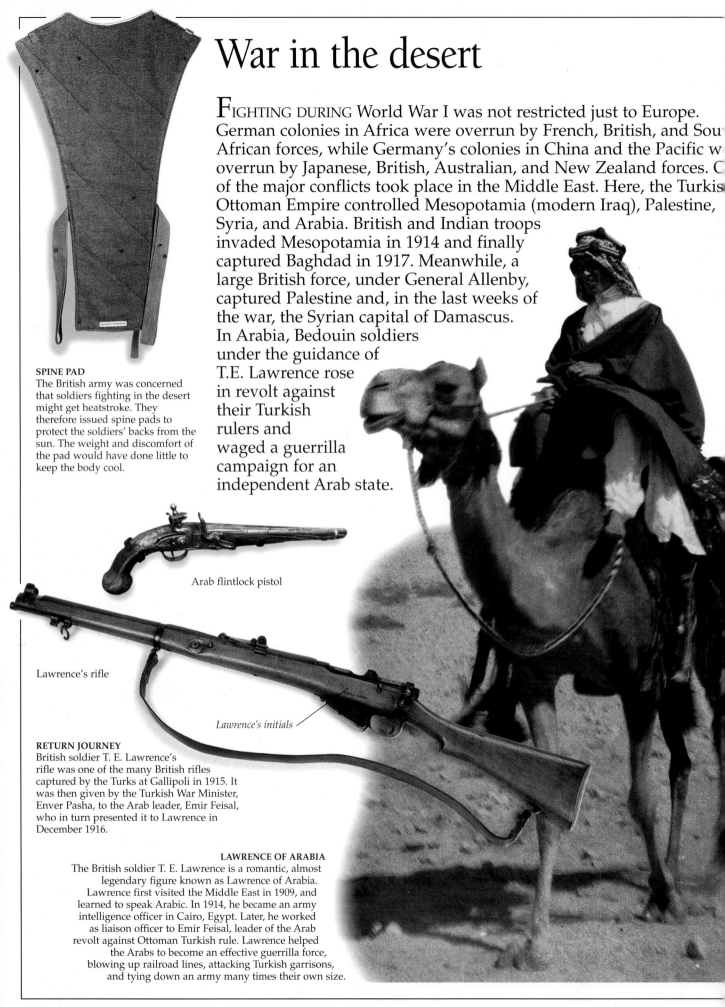

FIGHTING DURING World War I was not restricted just to Europe. German colonies in Africa were overrun by French, British, and Sou[th] African forces, while Germany's colonies in China and the Pacific w[ere] overrun by Japanese, British, Australian, and New Zealand forces. O[ne] of the major conflicts took place in the Middle East. Here, the Turkis[h] Ottoman Empire controlled Mesopotamia (modern Iraq), Palestine, Syria, and Arabia. British and Indian troops invaded Mesopotamia in 1914 and finally captured Baghdad in 1917. Meanwhile, a large British force, under General Allenby, captured Palestine and, in the last weeks of the war, the Syrian capital of Damascus. In Arabia, Bedouin soldiers under the guidance of T.E. Lawrence rose in revolt against their Turkish rulers and waged a guerrilla campaign for an independent Arab state.

SPINE PAD
The British army was concerned that soldiers fighting in the desert might get heatstroke. They therefore issued spine pads to protect the soldiers' backs from the sun. The weight and discomfort of the pad would have done little to keep the body cool.

Arab flintlock pistol

Lawrence's rifle

Lawrence's initials

RETURN JOURNEY
British soldier T. E. Lawrence's rifle was one of the many British rifles captured by the Turks at Gallipoli in 1915. It was then given by the Turkish War Minister, Enver Pasha, to the Arab leader, Emir Feisal, who in turn presented it to Lawrence in December 1916.

LAWRENCE OF ARABIA
The British soldier T. E. Lawrence is a romantic, almost legendary figure known as Lawrence of Arabia. Lawrence first visited the Middle East in 1909, and learned to speak Arabic. In 1914, he became an army intelligence officer in Cairo, Egypt. Later, he worked as liaison officer to Emir Feisal, leader of the Arab revolt against Ottoman Turkish rule. Lawrence helped the Arabs to become an effective guerrilla force, blowing up railroad lines, attacking Turkish garrisons, and tying down an army many times their own size.

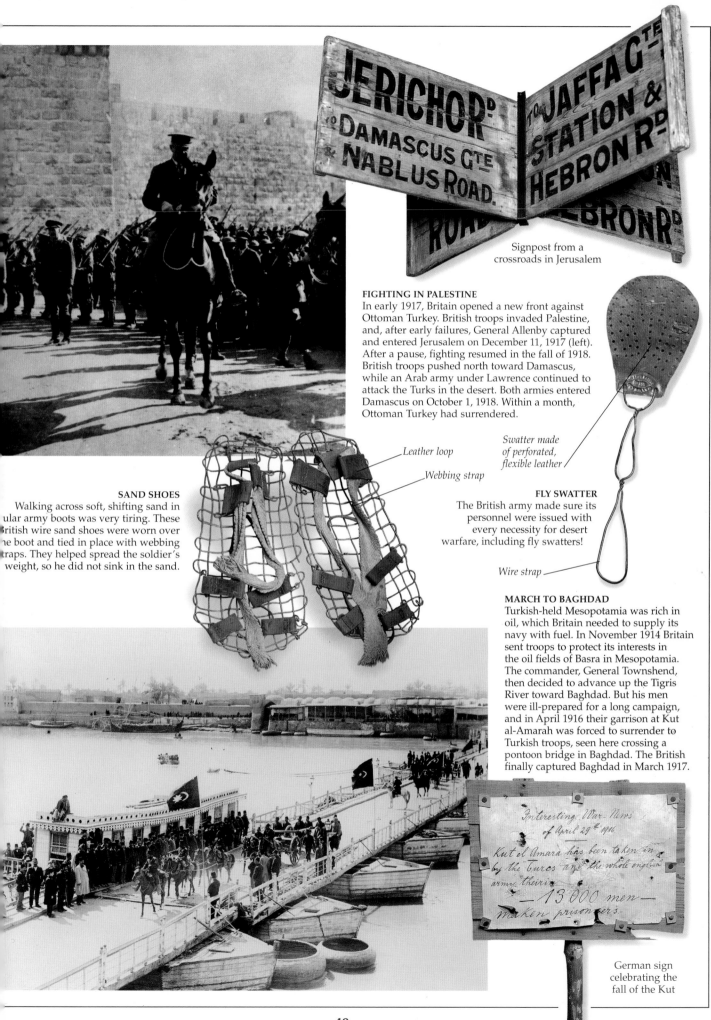

Signpost from a
crossroads in Jerusalem

FIGHTING IN PALESTINE

In early 1917, Britain opened a new front against
Ottoman Turkey. British troops invaded Palestine,
and, after early failures, General Allenby captured
and entered Jerusalem on December 11, 1917 (left).
After a pause, fighting resumed in the fall of 1918.
British troops pushed north toward Damascus,
while an Arab army under Lawrence continued to
attack the Turks in the desert. Both armies entered
Damascus on October 1, 1918. Within a month,
Ottoman Turkey had surrendered.

*Swatter made
of perforated,
flexible leather*

Leather loop

Webbing strap

FLY SWATTER

The British army made sure its
personnel were issued with
every necessity for desert
warfare, including fly swatters!

Wire strap

SAND SHOES

Walking across soft, shifting sand in
[reg]ular army boots was very tiring. These
[B]ritish wire sand shoes were worn over
[t]he boot and tied in place with webbing
[s]traps. They helped spread the soldier's
weight, so he did not sink in the sand.

MARCH TO BAGHDAD

Turkish-held Mesopotamia was rich in
oil, which Britain needed to supply its
navy with fuel. In November 1914 Britain
sent troops to protect its interests in
the oil fields of Basra in Mesopotamia.
The commander, General Townshend,
then decided to advance up the Tigris
River toward Baghdad. But his men
were ill-prepared for a long campaign,
and in April 1916 their garrison at Kut
al-Amarah was forced to surrender to
Turkish troops, seen here crossing a
pontoon bridge in Baghdad. The British
finally captured Baghdad in March 1917.

*Interesting War News
of April 29th 1916.
Kut el Amara has been taken in
by the Turcs and the whole english
army theirin
— 13 000 men —
Maken prisoners.*

German sign
celebrating the
fall of the Kut

Espionage

BOTH SIDES SUSPECTED the other of employing hundreds of spies to report on enemy intentions and capabilities. In fact, most espionage work consisted not of spying on enemy territory but of eavesdropping on enemy communications. Code-breaking or cryptography was very important as both sides sent and received coded messages by radio and telegraph. Cryptographers devised highly complex codes to ensure the safe transit of their own messages while using their skills to intercept and break coded enemy messages. Such skills enabled British intelligence to decipher the Zimmermann telegram from Berlin to Washington sent in January 1917, leading to the entry of the US into the war in April 1917.

Lightweight, but strong, string attaches parachute to bird

Corselet made of linen and padded to protect bird

POSTAL PIGEON
Over 500,000 pigeons were used during the war to carry messages between intelligence agents and their home bases. The pigeons were dropped by parachute into occupied areas. Agents collected the pigeons at drop zones and looked after them until they had information to send home. When released, the birds flew home to their lofts with messages attached to their legs.

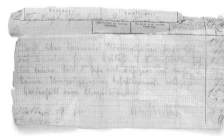

IN MINIATURE
Pigeons could not carry much weight, so messages had to be written on small pieces of paper. This message, in German, is written on a standard "pigeon post" form used by the German army. Long messages could be photographed with a special camera that reduced them to the size of a microdot – that is 300 hundred times smaller than the original.

EDITH CAVELL
Edith Cavell was born in England and worked as a governess in Belgium in the early 1890s before training in England as a nurse. In 1907 she returned to Belgium to start a nursing school in Brussels (above). When the Germans occupied the city in August 1914 she decided to stay, accommodating up to 200 British soldiers who also found themselves behind enemy lines. The Germans arrested her and tried her for "conducting soldiers to the enemy." She was found guilty and executed by firing squad in October 1915. Cavell was not a spy, but her execution did provide a powerful propaganda weapon for the Allies.

Front of button

Coded message on back of button

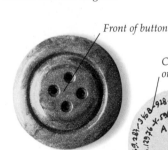

SECRET INK
Invisible ink was used to conceal messages written on paper. The invisible message could be read later when the paper was treated with a chemical to make the words visible.

German invisible ink and sponge

Invisible ink bottle

BUTTON MESSAGE
Coded messages could be written in the smallest and most unobtrusive of places. During the war, messages were stamped on the back of buttons sewn onto coats or jackets.

POCKET CAMERA
Small cameras hidden in a pocket or disguised as a pocket watch were used to take clandestine photographs. This spy camera was used in German East Africa (now Tanzania).

Lens cap

Camera lens

Shutter release

READING THE ENEMY
Army intelligence officers, such as this British soldier, played a vital role in examining and understanding captured enemy documents. Painstaking reading of every piece of information enabled the intelligence services to build up a reasonably complete picture about enemy preparations for an attack. They could also assess the state of civilian morale, and pass that information on to the military high command.

HIDDEN MESSAGES
Not every spy remained undetected. Two agents from the Netherlands sent to Portsmouth, England, to spy for Germany pretended to be cigar importers. They used their orders for imported Dutch cigars as codes for the ships they observed in Portsmouth harbor. They were caught and executed in 1915.

Cigars slit open in search of hidden messages

AID TO ESCAPE
This can, supposedly containing ox tongue, was sent to British Lieutenant Jack Shaw at the German prisoner of war camp, Holzminden in 1918. It contained maps, wire cutters, and compasses to help Shaw arrange a mass escape from the camp.

Rolled-up map of France

Lead weights to make the can the correct weight

Compass

MATA HARI
Dutch-born Margaretha Zelle was a famous dancer who used the stage name Mata Hari. She had many high-ranking lovers, which enabled her to pass on any confidential information she acquired from them to the secret services. In 1914, while dancing in Paris, she was recruited by the French intelligence service. She went to Madrid, where she tried to win over a German diplomat. He double-crossed her with false information, and on her return to France, she was arrested, tried, and found guilty of being a German agent. She was executed by firing squad in October 1917.

Tank warfare

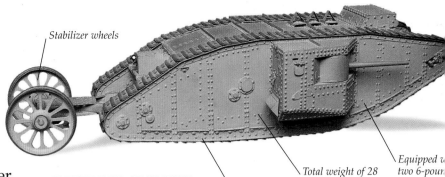

Stabilizer wheels

T HE BRITISH-INVENTED tank was a major mechanical innovation of the war. British tanks first saw action in 1916, but these early tanks were not very reliable. It was not until November 1917, at the Battle of Cambrai, that their full potential was realized. At Cambrai, the German defenses were so strong that an artillery bombardment would have destroyed the ground and made it impossible for the infantry to cross. Instead, fleets of tanks flattened barbed wire, crossed enemy trenches, and acted as shields for the advancing infantry. Tanks then played an important role in the allied advances throughout 1918.

Carried crew of eight men

Total weight of 28 tons (28,450 kg)

Equipped with two 6-pounder guns and machine g

BRITISH MARK 1 HEAVY TANK
The first tank to fight in battle was the British Mark 1 tank. Forty nine were ready to fight at the Battle of the Somme on September 15, 1916, but only 18 were reliable enough to take part in the battle itself.

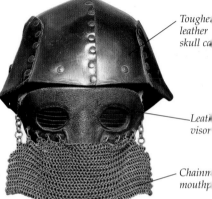

Toughe leather skull ca

Leath visor

Chainm mouthp

PROTECT AND SURVIVE
Leather helmets, faceguards, and chainmail mouthpieces were issued to British tank crews to protect their heads. The visors gave protection against particles of hot metal which flew off the inside of the hull when the tank was hit by a bullet.

German A7V tank

British MarkV tank

A7V TANK
The only German tank built during the war was the huge A7V, a 33-ton (33,500-kg) machine with six machine guns and a crew of 18. Only 20 A7Vs were constructed, and their appearance in the spring of 1918 was too late in the war to make any real impact.

...IDE A TANK

...inside a tank was very unpleasant. ...tank was hot, fume-ridden, and badly ...tilated, making the crew sick or even ...king them faint. The heat was ...etimes so great in light tanks that it ...loded the ammunition.

Rear entry hatch

Driver's entry hatch

Lid for driver's entry hatch

Driver's visor

T 9171

ME 9828

Iron caterpillar track

The driver and gunner were squashed in the front of the tank

Six men sat cramped around the engine manning the guns

Six-cylinder engine

BRITISH MARK V TANK
The British Mark V tank first fought in July 1918. It was equipped with two 6-pounder guns and four machine guns, and had a crew of eight. Its advanced system of gears and brakes allowed it to be driven and controlled by only one person.

Machine gun port

DRIVING A TANK
The first British tanks were driven by two people, each controlling one track. They had a limited range of 24 miles (40 km) and their tracks regularly broke. Later tanks were driven by a single person and were more maneuverable and robust. They were still vulnerable to enemy shellfire though, and often broke down, as here during the British assault on Arras in April 1917.

CROSSING THE TRENCHES
A tank could cross a narrow trench easily, but it could topple into a wide one. To solve this problem, the British equipped their tanks with circular metal bundles that could be dropped into a trench to form a bridge. Here, a line of Mark V tanks are moving in to attack German trenches in the fall of 1918.

The US enters the war

W<small>HEN WAR</small> broke out in Europe in August 1914, the US remained neutral. The country was deeply divided about the war, since many of its citizens had recently arrived from Europe and were strongly in favor of one side or the other. When German U-boats started to sink American ships, however, public opinion began to turn against Germany. In February 1917 Germany decided to attack all foreign cargo ships to try to reduce supplies to Britain. It also tried to divert US attention from Europe by encouraging its neighbor, Mexico, to invade. This action outraged the US government, and as more US ships were sunk, President Wilson declared war on Germany. This was now a world war.

British medal suggesting the attack on SS Lusitania was planned

SS LUSITANIA
On May 7, 1915, the passenger ship SS Lusitania was sunk off the coast of Ireland by German torpedoes because the ship was suspected of carrying munitions. The ship was bound from New York to Liverpool, England. Three quarters of the passengers drowned, including 12 US citizens. Their deaths did much to turn the US public against Germany and toward the Allies.

UNCLE SAM
The artist James Montgomery Flagg used himself as a model for Uncle Sam, a cartoon figure intended to represent every American. The portrait was based on Kitchener's similar pose for British recruiting posters (see page 14). Beneath his pointing finger were the words "I WANT YOU FOR THE US ARMY."

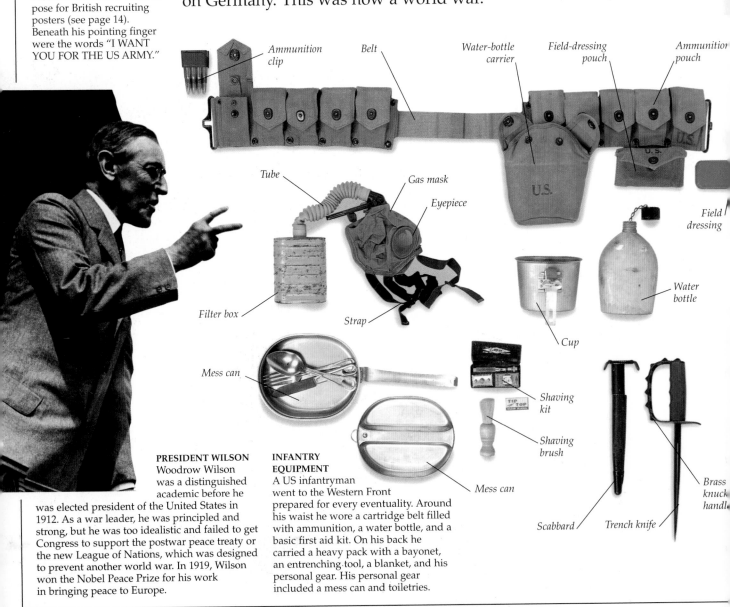

Ammunition clip

Belt

Water-bottle carrier

Field-dressing pouch

Ammunition pouch

Tube

Gas mask

Eyepiece

Field dressing

Filter box

Strap

Water bottle

Cup

Mess can

Shaving kit

Shaving brush

Mess can

Scabbard

Trench knife

Brass knuckle handle

PRESIDENT WILSON
Woodrow Wilson was a distinguished academic before he was elected president of the United States in 1912. As a war leader, he was principled and strong, but he was too idealistic and failed to get Congress to support the postwar peace treaty or the new League of Nations, which was designed to prevent another world war. In 1919, Wilson won the Nobel Peace Prize for his work in bringing peace to Europe.

INFANTRY EQUIPMENT
A US infantryman went to the Western Front prepared for every eventuality. Around his waist he wore a cartridge belt filled with ammunition, a water bottle, and a basic first aid kit. On his back he carried a heavy pack with a bayonet, an entrenching tool, a blanket, and his personal gear. His personal gear included a mess can and toiletries.

GUN FIRE
The US First Army saw its first major action on September 12–16, 1918 in St. Mihiel, south of Verdun, France, as part of a combined Allied attack against German lines. Here, an artillery crew fires a 3-in (75-mm) field gun as a spent shell casing flies through the air.

FOR HEROISM
Instituted by Presidential Order in 1918, the Distinguished Service Cross was awarded to someone for extreme heroism against an armed enemy.

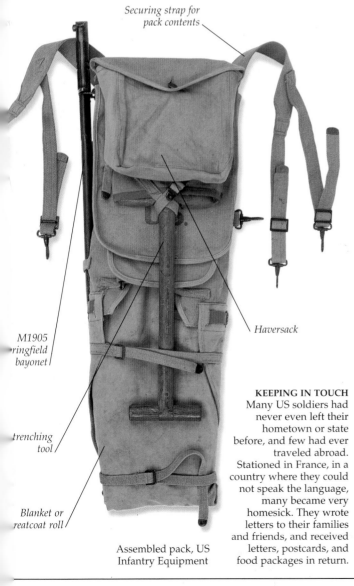

Securing strap for pack contents

Haversack

M1905 Springfield bayonet

trenching tool

Blanket or greatcoat roll

Assembled pack, US Infantry Equipment

KEEPING IN TOUCH
Many US soldiers had never even left their hometown or state before, and few had ever traveled abroad. Stationed in France, in a country where they could not speak the language, many became very homesick. They wrote letters to their families and friends, and received letters, postcards, and food packages in return.

Under enemy lines

TO THE RESCUE
A gas attack or a shell burst near a tunnel entrance could fill the mine with fumes, suffocating the men working inside. This German breathing apparatus was kept on standby for use by rescue parties.

Air tubes

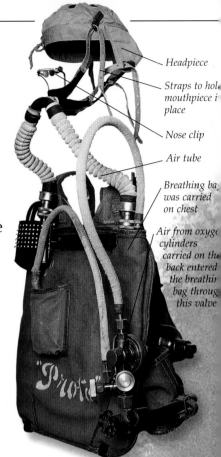

Headpiece

*Straps to hol
mouthpiece i
place*

Nose clip

Air tube

*Breathing ba
was carried
on chest*

*Air from oxyge
cylinders
carried on the
back entered
the breathin
bag throug
this valve*

OXYGEN RELIEF
This British breathing apparatus is similar to the German equipment on the left. Compressed oxygen contained in the breathing bags was released through the air tubes to help the miner breathe.

FOR MUCH OF the war on the Western Front, the two sides faced each other in rows of heavily fortified trenches. These massive defenses were very difficult to overcome, so engineers found ways of undermining them. The British army recruited coal miners and "clay kickers," who used to dig tunnels for the London subway system. The Germans had their own miners. Both excavated tunnels and mines deep under enemy lines and packed them with explosives, ready to be detonated when an attack began. Countermines were also dug to cut into and destroy enemy mines before they could be finished. The opposing miners sometimes met and fought in underground battles. Vast mines were exploded by the British at the Battle of the Somme on July 1, 1916, but their most effective use was under Messines Ridge at the start of the Battle of Passchendaele.

SAPPERS AT WORK
British artist David Bomberg's painting shows members of the Royal Engineers, known as sappers, digging and reinforcing an underground trench. Sappers ensured that trenches and tunnels were properly constructed and did not collapse.

Background picture: One of many British mines explodes under German lines at the Battle of the Somme, July 1, 1916

> *"It is horrible. You often wish you were dead, there is no shelter, we are lying in water ... our clothes do not dry."*
>
> GERMAN SOLDIER, PASSCHENDAELE, 1917

WATERLOGGED
The water table around Ypres was very high, so the trenches were built above ground by banking up soil and sand bangs. Even so, the trenches were constantly flooded. Pumping out mines and trenches, as these Australian tunnelers are doing at Hooge, Belgium, during September 1917, was an essential, never-ending task.

Passchendaele

During 1917, the British planned a massive attack against the German front line around Ypres, Belgium. They aimed to break into Belgium and capture the channel ports, stopping the German submarines from using them as a base to attack British shipping. The battle began on June 7, 1917.

After a huge artillery bombardment, 19 mines packed with 1 million tons of explosive blew up simultaneously under the German lines on Messines Ridge. The noise could be heard in London 140 miles (220 km) away. The ridge was soon captured, but the British failed to take quick advantage. Heavy rainfall in August and October turned the battlefield into a muddy wasteland. The village and ridge of Passchendaele were eventually captured on November 10, 1917, only to be lost again the following March. In summer of 1918, the Allies recaptured and kept the ground.

MUDDY QUAGMIRE
Heavy rainfall and constant shelling at Passchendaele created a deadly mudbath. Many injured men died when they were unable to lift themselves clear of the cloying mud. Stretcher-bearers were barely able to carry the wounded to dressing stations. The British poet Siegfried Sassoon wrote, "I died in hell – (They called it Passchendaele)."

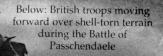

Below: British troops moving forward over shell-torn terrain during the Battle of Passchendaele

The final year

German and Russian troops celebrating the cease-fire on the Eastern Front, 1917

Russia pulls out

The Russian government became increasingly unpopular as the war progressed. The army was demoralized by constant defeats, and by early 1917, there was large-scale fraternization with German troops along the Eastern Front. In February 1917, a revolution overthrew the czar, but the new government continued the war. A second revolution in October brought the Bolshevik Party to power. A cease-fire was agreed with Germany, and in March 1918 Russia signed the Treaty of Brest-Litovsk and withdrew from the war.

THE LUDENDORFF OFFENSIVE
On March 21, 1918, General Ludendorff launched a huge attack on the Western Front. He hoped to defeat Britain and France before US reinforcements could arrive. The attack took the Allies by surprise, and Germany advanced by almost 40 miles (64 km) by July, but at the heavy cost of 500,000 casualties.

IN EARLY 1918, the war looked to be turning in favor of Germany and its allies. Russia had withdrawn from the war, enabling Germany to concentrate its efforts on the Western Front, and US troops had yet to arrive in France in any great numbers. A vast offensive in March brought German troops to within 40 miles (64 km) of Paris. But behind the lines, Germany was far from strong. The Allied blockade of German ports meant that the country was short of vital supplies. The railroad network was collapsing through lack of maintenance, and food was short. Strikes and even mutinies became common. Elsewhere, Ottoman Turkey and Bulgaria collapsed in the face of Allied attacks, while the Italians scored a decisive victory against Austria-Hungary. By early November, Germany stood alone. On November 7, a German delegation crossed the front line to discuss peace terms with the Allies. The war was almost over.

French and British troops in action during the Ludendorff Offensive

January 8 US President Wilson issues 14 Points for Peace
March 3 Treaty of Brest-Litovsk – Russia leaves the war
March 21 Vast German Ludendorff

offensive on the Western Front
July 15 Last German offensive launched on Western Front
July 18 French counterattack begins on the Marne

August 8 British launch offensive near Amiens
September 12 Americans launch offensive at St. Mihiel
September 14 Allies attack

Bulgaria from Greece
September 25 Bulgaria seeks peace
September 27 British begin to breach Hindenburg Line

BATTLE OF THE MARNE

On July 18, 1918, French and US forces, led by General Foch, counterattacked against the German advance on the Marne River, east of Paris. They stopped the German offensive in its tracks and began to push the Germans back eastward. By August 6, the Germans had lost 168,000 men, many buried where they fell on the battlefields (left). The tide of battle had at last turned decisively in favor of the Allied armies.

French soldiers identifying German dead before burial

CROSSING THE LINE

On August 8, 1918, a massive British offensive began near Amiens. The German army was increasingly short of men and vital supplies, including food, so gave little resistance. The Allied troops continued to push forward toward the heavily fortified Hindenburg Line, which had been built by the Germans as a fall-back defensive position. On September 29, the British 46th North Midland Division captured the bridge at Riqueval, over the St. Quentin Canal. They posed for a celebratory photograph, because they had broken the Line at last.

Many French children did not remember life before the German occupation of their towns and cities

Background picture: German troops advancing at the Somme, April 1918

French children march alongside the Allied army

THE LAST DAYS

By October 5, the Allied armies had breached the entire Hindenburg Line and were crossing open country. Both sides suffered great casualties as the German army was pushed steadily eastward. The British and French recaptured towns and cities lost in 1914, including Lille (left), and by early November 1918 they recaptured Mons, where they had fired the first shots of the war in August 1914. By now, the German retreat was turning into a rout.

...tember 28 German commander ...dendorff advises the Kaiser to seek ...ce as army crumbles
...ober 1 British capture Ottoman ...kish-held Damascus

October 6 German government starts to negotiate an armistice
October 21 Czechoslovakia declares its independence
October 24 Italian army begins

decisive battle of Vittorio-Veneto against Austria-Hungary
October 29 German fleet mutinies
October 30 Ottoman Turkey agrees an armistice

November 4 Austria-Hungary agrees an armistice
November 9 The Kaiser abdicates
November 11 Armistice between Germany and the Allies; war ends

Armistice and peace

CARRIAGE TALKS
On November 7, 1918, a German delegation headed by a government minister, Matthias Erzberger, crossed the front line to meet the Allied commander-in-chief, Marshal Foch, in his railroad carriage in the forest of Compiègne. At 5 am on November 11, the two sides signed an armistice agreement to come into effect six hours later.

Aт 11 AM ON THE 11th day of the 11th month of 1918, the guns of Europe fell silent after more than four years of war. The problems of war were now replaced by the equally pressing problems of peace. Germany had asked for an armistice (cease-fire) in order to discuss a possible peace treaty. It had not surrendered, but its soldiers were surrendering in hordes and its navy had mutinied. The Allies wanted to make sure that Germany would never go to war again. The eventual peace treaty redrew the map of Europe and forced Germany to pay massive damages to the Allies. German armed forces were reduced in size and strength, and Germany lost a great deal of land and all of its overseas colonies.

The New York Times.

**ARMISTICE SIGNED, END OF THE WAR!
BERLIN SEIZED BY REVOLUTIONISTS;
NEW CHANCELLOR BEGS FOR ORDER;
OUSTED KAISER FLEES TO HOLLAND**

DISPLACED PEOPLE
Many refugees, like these Lithuanians, were displaced during the war. The end of hostilities allowed thousands of refugees – mainly French, Belgians, Italians, and Serbians whose lands had been occupied by the Central Powers – to return home to their newly liberated countries. In addition, there were as many as 6.5 million prisoners of war who needed to be repatriated. This complex task was finally achieved by the fall of 1919.

SPREADING THE NEWS
News of the armistice spread around the world in minutes. It was reported in newspapers and typed out in telegrams, while word-of-mouth spread the joyous news to each and every member of the local neighborhood.

VIVE LA PAIX!
In Paris (below), French, British, and American soldiers joined Parisians in an impromptu procession through the city. In London, women and children danced in the streets, while their men prepared to return from the front. In Germany, the news was greeted with a mixture of shock and relief that the fighting was at last over.

THE TREATY OF VERSAILLES
[T]he peace treaty that ended the war was signed in [the] Hall of Mirrors in the Palace of Versailles near [Pari]s, on June 28, 1919. Sir William Orpen's painting [sho]ws the four Allied leaders watching the German [dele]gates sign the treaty ending German imperial [pow]er in Europe, just 48 years after the German [Emp]ire had been proclaimed in the same hall.

THE PEACE TREATIES
The Treaty of Versailles was signed by representatives of the Allied powers and Germany. The Allies signed subsequent treaties elsewhere in Paris with Austria in September 1919, Bulgaria in November 1919, Turkey in April 1920, and Hungary in June 1920. By then, a new map of Europe had emerged.

SIGNING THE TREATY
These soldiers watching the signing of the Treaty of Versailles had waited a long time for this moment. The Allies first met their German counterparts in January 1919. The Americans wanted a fair and just treaty that guaranteed democracy and freedom to all people, while both France and to a lesser extent Britain wanted to keep Germany weak and divided. Negotiations almost broke down several times before a final agreement was reached in June 1919.

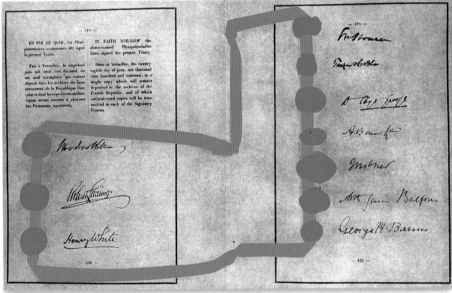

The Treaty of Versailles

Georges
Clemenceau

David
Lloyd
George

Vittorio
Orlando

Giorgio
Sonnino

[G]eneral
Foch

THE VICTORIOUS ALLIES
The negotiations in Paris were dominated by French premier Georges Clemenceau (supported by General Foch), British premier David Lloyd George, Italian premier Vittorio Orlando – seen here with his foreign minister, Giorgio Sonnino – and the US president Woodrow Wilson. Together the Big Four, as the leaders became known, thrashed out the main details of the peace settlement.

The cost of the war

THE COST OF THE World War I in human lives is unimaginable. More than 65 million men fought, of whom more than half were killed or injured – 8 million killed, 2 million died of illness and disease, 21.2 million wounded, and 7.8 million taken prisoner or missing. In addition, about 6.6 million civilians perished. Among the combatant nations, with the exception of the US, there was barely a family that had not lost at least one son or brother; some had lost every male member. Entire towns and villages were wiped off the map, and fertile farmland was turned into a deathly bogland. Financially, the economies of Europe were ruined, while the US emerged as a major world power. Not surprisingly, at the end of 1918, people hoped they would never again have to experience the slaughter and destruction they had lived through for the past four years.

ONE LIFE
A soldier stands on Pilckem Ridge during the Battle of Passchendaele in August 1917. The crudely made cross indicates a hastily dug grave, but many soldiers were engulfed by the mud and their graves remained unmarked.

THE UNKNOWN SOLDIER
Many of the dead were so badly disfigured that it was impossible to identify them. Plain crosses mark their graves. Thousands more just disappeared, presumed dead. Both France and Britain ceremoniously buried one unknown warrior – at the Arc de Triomphe, Paris, and Westminster Abbey, London.

AFTER CARE
The war left thousands of soldiers disfigured and disabled. Reconstructive surgery was carried out to repair facial damage, but masks were used to cover the most horrific disfigurement. Artificial limbs gave many disabled soldiers some mobility. But the horrors of the war remained forever.

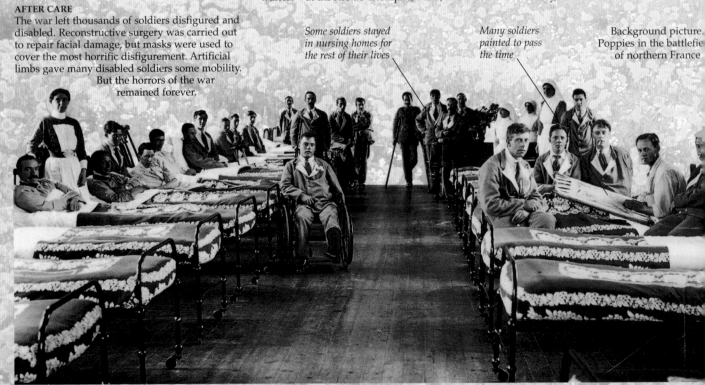

Some soldiers stayed in nursing homes for the rest of their lives

Many soldiers painted to pass the time

Background picture. Poppies in the battlefie of northern France

WAR MEMORIALS

The entire length of the Western Front is marked with graveyards and memorials to those who lost their lives in the war. The French national mausoleum and ossuary (burial vault) at Douaumont, Verdun (below), contains the remains of 130,000 unidentified French and German soldiers. There are 410 British cemeteries in the Somme valley alone.

Victoria
Cross
(V.C.)

FOR GALLANTRY

Every combatant nation awarded military and civilian medals to honor bravery. Five million Iron Crosses were given to German soldiers and their allies. Over two million Croix de Guerre were issued to French soldiers, military units, civilians, and towns, and 576 Victoria Crosses, Britain's highest award, were presented to British and Empire troops.

French *Croix de Guerre*

..MENTOS

..ofusion of flowers, including red Flanders poppies, ..r along both sides of the Western Front. Soldiers, such ..rivate Jack Mudd of the 214 Battalion of the London ..ment (above), would press them as mementos to send ..e to their loved ones. Mudd sent this poppy to his .. Lizzie before he was killed, in 1917, in the Battle of ..chendaele. Canadian doctor, John McCrae, wrote the ..n *In Flanders Fields* after tending wounded soldiers near ..s in 1915. His mention of poppies in the poem inspired ..British Legion to sell paper poppies to raise money for ..ed soldiers, and as a sign of remembrance for the dead.

Did you know?

BITE-SIZED FACTS

The noise produced by artillery barrages and mines was incredibly loud. In 1917, explosives blowing up beneath the German lines on Messines Ridge at Ypres in Belgium could be heard in London, 140 miles (220 km) away.

Every British soldier was given army-issue boots in time to wear them in. From the Somme onward, each soldier also had his own steel helmet. Specialized items, such as rubber waders, were kept as communal stores—handed from one unit to another.

British Army clothing, left to right: a warm coat for transport drivers; a flameproof suit for flame thrower operators; winter camouflage for trench raiding; and flying clothing

Flame throwers were first used by the Germans. They fired jets of flame as far as 130 ft (40 m).

Russia had the largest army. It mobilized 12 million troops during the course of the war. More than three-quarters were killed, wounded, or went missing in action.

At first British tanks were split into "males" and "females." Male tanks had cannons, while females had heavy machine guns.

The first prototype tank, "Little Willie," was built in 1915. It carried a crew of three and had a top speed of 3 mph (4.8 km/h).

Tunnelers laid mines on the Western Front. Sometimes underground fights broke out, if they dug into an enemy tunnel by mistake.

Map of Europe in 1914 by Walter Trier

Food was prepared in field kitchens that could be several miles behind the front line. It was impossible to take transportation into the trench, so food was carried to the front on foot.

Filling a Thermos container that kept the food hot

Prague-born Walter Trier (1890–1951) produced political cartoons. One famous work shows Europe in 1914 on the eve of World War I, with the national leaders squabbling and threatening each other.

The Pool of Peace is a 40-ft (12-m) deep lake near Messines, Belgium. It fills a crater made in 1917 when the British detonated a mine containing 45 tons (41,325 kg) of explosives.

Some soldiers wore knitted helmets called balaclavas to stay warm in the winter. Balaclavas are named after the battle where they were first worn—the Battle of Balaclava, which took place during the Crimean War (1854).

A German messenger dog laying telegraph wire

Messenger dogs carried orders to the front line in capsules strapped to their bodies. Dogs also helped military communications in another way—some of them were trained to lay down telegraph wire!

QUESTIONS AND ANSWERS

Modern-day camouflage

Q Who was "Big Bertha"?

A Big Bertha was a 48-ton (43,700-kg) howitzer used by the Germans in World War I. Its designer, Gustav Krupp, named the weapon after his wife. Big Bertha was more mobile than the previous 16.5-in (420-mm) howitzer; it could be transported to its firing position by tractor. Even so, it took its crew of 200 men six hours or more to assemble it. Big Bertha was a formidable weapon. It could fire a 2,050-lb (930-kg) shell a distance of 9.3 miles (15 km). Big Bertha's first successes were at Liege in Belgium. The 12 forts ringing the city were destroyed in three days.

Q Why did soldiers keep animals?

A Most animals that traveled with the army had a job to do. Mules, horses, and camels were kept as draft or pack

Soldiers with their rabbits and chickens

animals to transport heavy supplies. Messenger dogs and pigeons carried important communications. Away from the front line, some soldiers kept animals for food—rabbits for the cooking pot or hens for their eggs. Some animals were kept simply to keep up morale. Dogs, for example, were popular, but one group of South African soldiers had an impala as its lucky mascot!

Q How did soldiers camouflage themselves?

A World War I was the first major conflict in which soldiers made use of camouflage. They wore khaki uniforms that blended in with the background. Some snipers made camouflaged suits out of painted sacking. Steel helmets were often painted with matte paint mixed with sand or sawdust so that they would not reflect the light; other times they were smeared with mud or covered with sacking from sandbags. Soldiers also used sacking or netting to hide their equipment from the reconnaissance aircraft patrolling the skies, but blending in was not the only camouflage possibility. The disruptive patterns painted on to battleships also worked—just as a zebra's stripes can confuse a lion.

Q How did soldiers know when to put on their gas masks?

A There were soldiers on lookout duty night and day. These sentries used whatever they could find to raise the alarm—bells, rattles, whistles, or just their own voice. When the soldiers heard the alarm they put on their gas masks as quickly as they could—hopefully before the deadly gas drifted toward the trench.

Q Why were tanks called tanks?

A While it was being developed, the tank was known as a "landship." However, there were fears that this name was too obvious. Before long, a German spy might become curious about why so many of these objects were being produced, and the Germans might catch on to the new invention. The British had to come up with a believable name. They decided that, with its rectangular body-shape, perhaps it could be passed off as a water storage tank. At first, they chose the name "water carrier"—until someone noticed that this would be abbreviated to "WC." In the end they decided on "tank" instead.

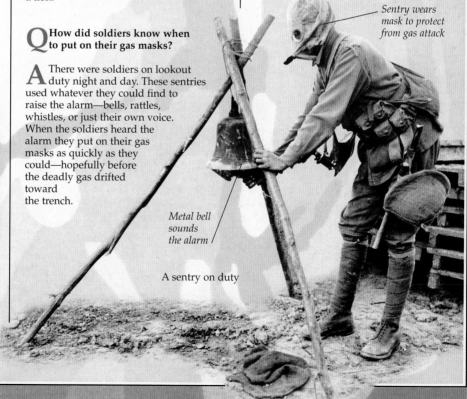

Sentry wears mask to protect from gas attack

Metal bell sounds the alarm

A sentry on duty

Key people and places

So many people played an important role in planning or fighting World War I. It is impossible to cover them all, but here are a few of them, together with a checklist of some of the key battle sites.

General Joseph Joffre

King George V of Britain

General Ferdinand Foch

IMPORTANT PERSONALITIES

President Raymond Poincaré of France

General Sir Douglas Haig

Russian General Brusilov

ALEXEI BRUSILOV (1853–1926)
With his "Brusilov offensive" of 1916, General Brusilov broke Austro-Hungarian lines. He took command of Russian armies on the Eastern Front in 1917.

LUIGI CADORNA (1850–1928)
The general in charge of the Italian army was Luigi Cadorna. His only success was the recapture of Gorizia in 1916.

FERDINAND FOCH (1851–1929)
Artillery specialist Ferdinand Foch successfully led the French at the Marne. By 1918 he was coordinating all the Allied forces on the Western Front.

ANTHONY FOKKER (1890–1939)
Dutch designer Anthony Fokker developed the first fighter plane with a forward-facing synchronized machine gun. His Fokker Eindecker gave Germany the edge in the early part of the war. Fokker produced 40 different aircrafts during the war.

RENÉ FONCK (1894–1953)
Frenchman René Fonck was the Allies' most successful fighter pilot. He shot down 75 enemy planes.

DOUGLAS HAIG (1861–1928)
The general in charge of British troops on the Western Front was Sir Douglas Haig. He ordered the offensives at the Somme and Passchendaele, as well as the final, successful Allied offensive.

PAUL VON HINDENBURG (1847–1934)
Early in the war, Paul von Hindenburg successfully led the Germans against the Russians. By 1916, he commanded all German land forces. His Hindenburg Line, created in 1917, withstood attack till 1918.

JOSEPH JOFFRE (1852–1931)
When the war broke out, Joseph Joffre became Commander of the French army. He planned attacks on the Western Front but, after heavy losses, was replaced in 1916.

T. E. LAWRENCE (1888–1935)
Known as Lawrence of Arabia, T. E. Lawrence worked for Allied intelligence in the Middle East. He led an Arab revolt against the Turks, which he wrote about in his book *The Seven Pillars of Wisdom*.

RITTMEISTER VON RICHTHOFEN (1892–1918)
Known as the Red Baron, this German aviator shot down 80 planes—more than any other World War I pilot. He died after being shot down near Amiens.

MAXIMILIAN VON SPEE (1861–1914)
German admiral Maximilian von Spee sank two British cruisers off Chile. He died when his own ship, the *Scharnhorst*, went down near the Falkland Islands.

GABRIEL VOISIN (1880–1973)
French-born Gabriel Voisin was an aircraft designer. He is famous for his Voisin III (the first Allied plane to shoot down an enemy) and his Voisin V bomber, which was armed with a cannon.

MARGARETHA ZELLE (1876–1917)
Dutch-born Margaretha Zelle was better known as Mata Hari. She always denied being a double agent, but it is possible that she spied for both the French and Germans. The French executed her in 1917.

Anthony Fokker with his Fokker D1 aircraft

Propeller rotation was synchronized with gunfire

Aircraft designer Gabriel Voisin (right)

Tanks pass through Meaulte, France, during the Amiens offensive

AMIENS
In August 1918, General Rawlinson led his successful Allied offensive to recapture the Amiens Line. On the first day, the Allies advanced 7.5 miles (12 km).

CAMBRAI
General Haig took the Germans by surprise in November 1917 when he attacked them at Cambrai, France. At first, the Allies gained good ground, but within two weeks the Germans had regained their position. The estimated casualties were 45,000 British soldiers and 50,000 Germans.

GAZA
General Dobell led a British attack on Turkish-held Gaza in March 1917. The port was a strategic target, on the way to Palestine. The British took the Turks by surprise, but were soon forced to retreat. They eventually captured Gaza in November, after weakening its defenses with bombardment from offshore ships.

A British dressing station at Cambrai

HELIGOLAND BIGHT
In August 1914, two British light cruisers and 25 destroyers attacked German ships near the naval base on Heligoland in the North Sea. In the battle that followed, the British sank three cruisers and a destroyer.

JUTLAND
May 1916 saw the war's only major sea battle, off the Danish coast of Jutland. Both sides claimed victory. The Germans inflicted the heaviest losses, but the British had maintained control of the North Sea.

The Retreat from Mons (1927) by Lady Elizabeth Butler

MONS
The British Expeditionary Force met the advancing German army at Mons, France, in August 1914. Although the Germans suffered heavy losses, they managed to force back the British to the Marne River.

PASSCHENDAELE
The Battle of Passchendaele, Belgium, began in July 1917. First, the Allies spent 10 days bombarding the Germans. Then they advanced, but were slowed down by torrential rains. The Allies finally took the ridge of Passchendaele in November.

SOMME
July 1916 saw the start of the Battle of the Somme, France. On the first day, the British suffered 58,000 casualties. Despite this, the Allies continued their offensive until November. When it was finally called off, the Allies had suffered 620,000 casualties and the Germans an estimated 500,000 casualties.

VERDUN
The Germans attacked the French garrison town of Verdun in February 1916. Initially they outnumbered the French five to one, but they failed to take the town. The battle ran on for 10 months and nearly a million men lost their lives.

VITTORIO-VENETO
One of the last offensives of the war was when the Italians recaptured Vittorio-Veneto on October 29, 1918. The Austro-Hungarian forces had retreated the day before.

YPRES
The Belgian town of Ypres was taken by the Germans in August 1914, but the British recaptured it in October. During the failed German counterattack, the British forces were decimated. A second battle of Ypres took place in April and May 1915 and a third, Passchendaele, in 1917.

A British field kitchen at the Somme, 1916

Find out more

THERE ARE MANY WAYS you can find out more about World War I. Ask older generations of your family if they remember stories about relatives who fought in the war. There are personal accounts online, too, plus lots of other information. Try your library for special books on the topic and visit war museums. In addition to vast collections of fascinating objects, these often have interactive displays. Television documentaries also bring the war to life with real or reconstructed footage. Finally, remember there is a wealth of old war films that will give you a feel for what life was like.

Poppy symbolizes remembrance

REMEMBRANCE DAY
Everyone can play a part in commemorating the sacrifices of soldiers and civilians during World War I. Each year, on the Sunday nearest to November 1, services are held at local and national war memorials.

THE TANK MUSEUM
Fans of tracked vehicles should head to Bovington, Dorset, England, to see the world's largest tank collection. A key attraction is the first tank prototype, Little Willie. The museum also has a program of special events.

ARC DE TRIOMPHE
Originally built by Napoleon to celebrate the victories of his armies, the Arc de Triomphe in Paris, France, now honors the memory of the millions of soldiers killed in World War I. Its flame of remembrance is rekindled each day and, in November 1920, the body of an unknown soldier was buried under the monument. He is there to symbolize the soldiers who died in the war.

Anzac veteran wears wartime medals and decorations

French tricolor (national flag) is flown each year on November 11

ANZAC DAY
If you are in Australia or New Zealand April 25 you will be able to take part Anzac Day. There are parades and ceremonies to mark the lives of the thousands of Australian and New Zealand soldiers who died at Gallipoli, Turkey, in 1915.

Places to visit

SMITHSONIAN INSTITUTION, WASHINGTON, D.C.
Explore the myths and realities of World War I combat. On exhibit are actual aircraft that took to the skies during World War I.

LIBERTY MEMORIAL MUSEUM, KANSAS CITY, MISSOURI
The only public museum in the United States dedicated solely to the history of World War I. Historical items in the collection include gas masks, letters and postcards from the field, memorial paintings, and other artifacts from World War I.

PARRIS ISLAND MUSEUM, PARRIS ISLAND, SOUTH CAROLINA
Marines were among the first forces to be sent to France during World War I. This World War I exhibit features foreign and domestic apparel, equipment, and weapons, including trench knives, a Maxim water-cooled machine gun, and a Model 1908 Luger used by the Germans.

THE US AIR FORCE (USAF) MUSEUM, DAYTON, OHIO
The history gallery provides an overview of the US Army Air Service involvement in World War I. The gallery supports actual displays of World War I aircraft at the largest military aviation museum in the world.

IMPERIAL WAR MUSEUM, LONDON, ENGLAND
See a World War I tank, or visit a dedicated gallery with firearms, uniforms, posters, medals, and other memorabilia in themed areas. The Trench Experience exhibit features sights, sounds, and smells that bring the Battle of the Somme to life.

FILMS

...reat many movies have ...n made about the events ...World War I. They may not ...ays be based on solid facts, ...they are an entertaining way ...et a flavor of the time and ...ts. One of the best ...wrence of Arabia (1962). ...cted by David Lean, it ...red Peter O'Toole (shown ...ve) in the title role.

USEFUL WEB SITES

- Easy-to-navigate site with reference library links to timelines, maps, and biographies:
  www.worldwar1.com/reflib.htm
- A companion Web site to the PBS series on World War I, including multimedia effects:
  www.pbs.org/greatwar
- The World Almanac for Kids' history timeline:
  www.worldalmanacforkids.com/EXPLORE/us_history/worldwar1.html

Life-size model shows army doctor dressing wounds

Sculpture shows parents mourning the loss of their son

WAR MONUMENT
Many artists and writers were so horrified or moved by the war that they felt compelled to express these feelings in their work. German sculptor Kathe Kollwitz (1867–1945) made this statue for the German war cemetery at Roggevelde, Belgium. Her own son, Peter, is buried there.

IMPERIAL WAR MUSEUM
This exhibit is part of the Trench Experience at the Imperial War Museum, London, England. A combination of lights, sounds, and smells helps visitors to understand just how terrifying and disorientating trench life was.

Glossary

Nurses wheel convalescent soldiers around the hospital grounds

ABDICATE To give up office or power

ALLIANCE A group of allies who have agreed to act in cooperation. Allied countries often set out their shared aims in an official treaty.

ALTITUDE Height above sea level

AMMUNITION Bullets and shells fired from weapons

AMPUTATION Surgical removal of a body part, such as an arm or leg

ANZAC Member of the Australian and New Zealand Army Corps

ARMISTICE End of hostilities. Armistice Day, now known as Veteran's Day or Remembrance Sunday, is commemorated each year on or around November 11.

ARMS RACE Competition between nations to build up weaponry or armaments

ARTILLERY Armed forces that use heavy weapons, such as cannons

ASSASSINATION The murder of someone for political purposes

BATTERY The place where a cannon, or other form of artillery, is positioned

BAYONET A blade attached to a rifle or other firearm. The bayonet can be used to stab the enemy at close quarters.

BULLY BEEF Another name for corned beef
BUNKER An underground bomb shelter

BUTTON STICK Metal slide used to protect a soldier's uniform while buttons are polished

CAMOUFLAGE Coloring designed to blend in with the background. During World War I, this was mostly limited to attempts to conceal gun positions, although some soldiers blackened their faces before night patrols and snipers wore camouflaged suits.

CAVALRY Originally, soldiers on horseback, but the term came to mean soldiers using motorized transport, such as tanks

CLIP A means of carrying and rapidly loading rifle ammunition

COLONY A dependency, or place, that is ruled by a foreign nation

CONSCIENTIOUS OBJECTOR Someone who refuses to fight in a war for moral reasons

CONSCRIPT Someone who is forced by law to fight in the army

CONSCRIPTION Making people fight in the army

Small box-respirator gas mask

CONVALESCENT Someone who has been seriously injured or ill and is slowly recovering

CONVOY Merchant ships traveling together, protected by a naval escort

CREEPING BARRAGE A line of artillery fire that moves slowly ahead of an infantry advance

CRYPTOGRAPHY The study and creation of secret codes

DETONATE To explode or cause to explode

DYSENTERY An infection of the intestines that causes diarrhea and bloody feces

EMPLACEMENT A mound or platform from which guns are fired

ENDEMIC Found in a particular area or among a certain group of people

ENLIST To sign up to join the armed forces

ENTENTE A friendly agreement or

An intelligence officer inspects aerial photographs of enemy trenches

informal alliance between nations

EVACUATION Moving people away from a place where they are in danger

FLOTILLA A fleet or group of small ships

FRONT LINE The border between enemy territories where the fighting takes place

FUSELAGE The body of an airplane

GAS In the context of war, "gas" means a poisonous gas, such as chlorine, used as a weapon to choke, blind, or kill the enemy

GRENADE A small bomb that is hurled by hand

GUERRILLA A soldier in a guerrilla

An American propaganda poster

TOGETHER WE WIN
UNITED STATES SHIPPING BOARD ▪▪▪ EMERGENCY FLEET CORPORATION

army—a small-scale outfit that practices sabotage and hit-and-run attacks. Guerrilla comes from the Spanish for "small war."

HOWITZER A short gun that fires high

INCENDIARY Describes a bomb, bullet, or other device designed to cause fire

INFANTRY Foot soldiers

INTELLIGENCE Useful

British .303-in (7.7-mm) Maxim Mark 3 medium machine gun, c. 1902

military or political information, or the spies that gather it

INTERROGATE To question someone aggressively

KNOT A unit for measuring a ship's speed. One knot equals 1.15 mph (1.85 km/h).

MACHINE GUN An automatic gun that fires bullets in rapid succession

MEDICAL ORDERLY A soldier with some medical training who works in an army medical establishment

MESS TIN A soldier's cooking pot

MINE A large underground chamber packed with explosives, which is placed under enemy lines by tunnelers

MOBILIZATION Preparation of troops for active service

MORALE Strength of purpose, confidence, or faith

MORSE CODE A code where each letter of the alphabet is represented by a sequence of dots and dashes, or by long or short signals of light or sound. It is named after its inventor, Samuel Morse (1791–1872).

MUNITIONS Stores of weapons

NEUTRALITY The state of not taking sides

NO-MAN'S-LAND An area of land between two opposing forces that has not been captured by either side

NONCOMBATANT Someone connected with the army but not there to fight, for example, a chaplain or army doctor

PERISCOPE A device that uses mirrors to allow the user to see things that are not in his or her direct line of sight

PICQUET A metal stake used to tether an entanglement—that is, a tangle of barbed wire used to fortify the front-row trenches

POSTHUMOUSLY After death

PROPAGANDA Information intended to convince people of a particular viewpoint. It may take the form of posters, broadcasts, or air-dropped leaflets, for example.

PUTTEE A strip of cloth wound around the lower part of the leg

RECONNAISSANCE Taking a preliminary look at an area before sending in troops, usually in order to locate the enemy

RECONNOITER

German stereoscopic periscope

To survey an area in preparation for a military advance

RECRUIT Someone who is enlisted into the army

REGULAR FORCES Soldiers who already belong to the army, rather than conscripts

RESERVE FORCES People who are not part of the regular army but have received some military training and are ready to be the first extra troops mobilized in an emergency

RESPIRATOR A device worn over the face to prevent the wearer from breathing in poison gas

RIFLE A long-barreled gun, fired from shoulder level

SEAPLANE An aircraft equipped with floats or skis so that it can land on or take off from water

SHELL An explosive device that is fired, for example from a cannon.

SHELLSHOCK Mental strain or illness suffered by a soldier who has fought in a war

SHRAPNEL A type of antipersonnel projectile that contains small shot or spherical bullets, usually of lead, along with an explosive charge to scatter the shot

TELEGRAPH A communications device that transmits messages by means of electrical signals along a wire

TERRORIST Someone who commits violent acts to bring about or draw attention to his or her political aims

TORPEDO A self-propelled underwater missile that can be fired from a boat or submarine

TRENCH A ditch dug by soldiers that gives some protection against enemy fire

TRUCE An agreement to stop fighting

U-BOAT A German submarine

ULTIMATUM A final demand that, if not met, will result in serious consequences

WAR BOND A certificate issued by a government in return for the investment of a sum of money. The money raised by the bonds helps pay for the war.

WAR OF ATTRITION Continuously attacking to wear down the enemy.

Index

Acknowledgments

Dorling Kindersley and the author would like to thank: Elizabeth Bowers, Christopher Dowling, Mark Pindelski, & the photography archive team at the Imperial War Museum for their invaluable help; Right Section, Kings Own Royal Horse Artillery for firing the gun shown on page 10; Lynn Bresler for the index.

For this edition, the publishers would also like to thank: the author for assisting with revisions; Claire Bowers, David Ekholm–JAlbum, Sunita Gahir, Joanne Little, Nigel Ritchie, Susan St Louis, Carey Scott, & Bulent Yusef for the clip art; David Ball, Neville Graham, Rose Horridge, Joanne Little, & Susan Nicholson for the wall chart.

The publishers would also like to thank the following for their kind permission to reproduce their photographs:
a=above, b=below, c=center, l=left, r=right, t=top

AKG London: 6l, 7crb, 36br, 37bl, 38cl, 38bl, 41tr, 42c, 42bl, 43br, 38cl, 38bl, 41tr, 42c, 42bl, 43br, 52cl,

58–59t, 60c. Bovington Tank Museum: 68ca. Bridgeman Art Library, London/New York: © Royal Hospital Chelsea, London, UK 67tr. Corbis: 2tr, 6tr, 7tr, 20tr, 22tr, 31tr; Bettmann 8tr, 26–27, 44–45c, 49bl, 55tr, 35bc, 49tl, 54bl, 55t, 55br, 58–59, 61cr, 69br; Randy Faris 64–65; Christel Gerstenberg 64tr; Dallas and John Heaton 68bl; Dave G. Houser 41cr; © Hulton-Deutsch Collection 66br; Michael St Maur Sheil 70–71 bckgrd; Swim Ink 71tl. DK Picture Library: Andrew L. Chernack, Springfield, Pennsylvania: 3tr, 55tr; Imperial War Museum 2cr, 13cl, 20bl, 20br, 27bc, 28cl, 41c, 50bc, 51c, 70bc, 71tr, 71bl, 71br; National Army Museum: 44bl; RAF Museum, Hendon: 34cla, 34cl; Spink and Son Ltd: 3tl, 4tr, 43bc. Robert Harding Picture Library: 63c. Heeresgeschichtliches Museum, Wien: 8bl. Hulton Getty: 14tl, 17tl, 19br, 21br, 33tr, 32–33b, 35clb, 36cra, 41c, 43t, 47cra, 50clb, 51cl, 58tl, 60tl, 60b, 61tr, 61b; Topical Press Agency 50cl. Imperial War Museum: 2tl, 8tl (HU68062), 9bl (Q81763), 11tr (Q70075), 10–11t (Q70232), 12clb (32002), 14bc

(Q42033), 15tr (Cat. No. 0544), 15cr (Q823), 16c (Q57228), 16b (Q193), 17br (E(AUS)577), 18tr (CO2533), 18cl (Q2953), 18cr (IWM90/62/6), 18br (IWM90/62/4), The Menin Road by Paul Nash 19tr (Cat. No. 2242), 19cla, 19cr, 19clb (Q872), 21tc (IWM90/62/5), 21tr (IWM90/62/3), 22bca, 22bl (CO1414), 23t (Q1462), 23br (Q8477), 24tl (Q54985), 24c, 26bl (Q104), 27tl (E921), 26–27b (Q3214), 28cr, 29tr (Q1561), 29br (Q739), 28–29b (Q53), 30tr (Q1778), 30cl (Q2628), 31br (Q4502), 32l, 32c (Q8537), 33tl (Q30678), 33tr (1646), 33cr (Q19134), 35cb (Q42284), 35bl (Q69593), 34–35c, 36clb, 37 (Q27488), 38tl, 38tr (PST0515), 39cr (Q20883), 39br (Q63698), 40cl (Q13618), 40br (Q13281), 41tl (Q13603), 41b (Q13637), 45br (Q55085), Gassed by John Singer Sargent 44–45b (1460), 48cr (Q60212), 48bl, 51tr (Q26945), 52bl (Q9364), 53cr (Q6434), 53br (Q9364), 54tl (2747), Sappers at Work by David Bomberg 56cl (2708), 57tr (E(AUS)1396), 57cr (Q5935), 56–57c (Q754), 56–57b (Q1938), 58b (Q10810), 59tr (Q9534), 59b (Q9586), The Signing of Peace in the Hall of Mirrors, Versailles by Sir William Orpen 61tl (2856), 62tl (Q2756), 62c (Q1540), 64cla (Q30788), 64crb (Q50671), 64bc (Q4834), 65clb (Q10956), 65br (Q609), 66tr

(Q949), 66cla (Q54534), 66bl (Q66377), 67tl (Q7302), 67clb (Q9631), 67br (Q1582), 69bl (IWM 90-62-3), 70tl (Q27814), 70cr (Q26946); David King Collection: 46bl, 47tl, 58cla. Kobal Collection: Columbia 69tl. National Gallery Of Canada, Ottawa: Transfer from the Canadian War Memorials, Dazzle ships in dry dock at Liverpool, 1921 by Edward Wadsworth 39tl. Peter Newark's Military Pictures: 13ac, 42tr. Pa Photos: European Press Agency 65t. Popperfoto: Reuters 68br. Roger-Viollet: 9tr, 9cr, 11br, 13cr, 19tl; Boyer 17bl. Telegraph Colour Library: J.P. Fruchet 62c. Topham Picturepoint: 42tl, 46tl, 47br, 46–47b, 62b; ASAP 43cl. Ullstein Bild: 8–9c, 46tr.

Wall chart: Corbis: Bettmann br, tr

Jacket credits: Front: Corbis, b; Imperial War Museum, UK, cl; Spink and Son Ltd, UK, tcl; Swim Ink/Corbis, tc. Back: Imperial War Museum, tl, cl, c, bc, cr.

All other images © Dorling Kindersley.
For further information see:
www.dkimages.com